THE CREATIVE WRITING STUDENT'S HANDBOOK

Cathie Hartigan and Margaret James

cwm

TABLE OF CONTENTS

How do you become a successful writer?

You'll need commitment, passion, determination and a good teacher.

But you'll also need to be a good learner.

As teachers of creative writing, we have had the huge pleasure of seeing many of our students achieve publication and win or be shortlisted for prizes. Our students have become confident, articulate writers who have learned to use their own special talents to their maximum potential.

We notice that the students who are most likely to succeed are those who enjoy engaging in all aspects of the writing process and are also good learners - who listen, are willing to take direction and are open to suggestion. Good learners are happy to take part in constructive discussions and have plenty to offer the teacher in the way of student feedback.

Our aim is to help you to discover the pleasures of creative writing and become a successful writer yourself.

CHAPTER 1

What a creative writing teacher can and can't do

A creative writing teacher can:

Inspire you
Enable you to find your writing voice
Help you to improve
Provide you with information

A creative writing teacher can't:

Tell you what to write
Write it for you
Guarantee publication or competition success
Save your life

Inspiration

Human beings love stories. They like to tell, hear, read and write them. Stories are one of the ways in which we respond to, make sense of and communicate with the world.

Creative writing teachers are usually writers themselves. But they don't have to be bestselling or prizewinning novelists. They need to be committed and enthusiastic teachers. A teacher with a passion for the subject can be hugely inspirational. So that's the sort of teacher you'll need to find.

All creative writing teachers should encourage you to read widely. They should also tell you that reading the sort of story you want to write is essential. So don't listen to people who say: don't read this or that because you might be influenced by its style or content. Of course you might be influenced.

When you admire (or shudder at the very thought of) other people's houses – their decor, their furniture or their DVD collections – this can be an enriching experience.

Perhaps you'll think: a sofa like Jane's would look grand in my sitting room. But fancy putting it with that carpet! A sheepskin would look much better. Or perhaps a Chinese rug? I wouldn't have blue walls, I'd have green.

Soon, you'll have a whole new imaginary room. It isn't like Jane's, but it does have a splendid sofa which *is* the same as hers. Strangely, this sofa looks quite different in your room.

If you lived on a desert island with nothing but the complete works of Shakespeare to read, it's likely your own writing style would come to reflect his. It's a fact that much of what Shakespeare wrote still enhances and enriches our language. Some of his expressions are now so commonplace that we think of them as clichés – for example: *this is the long and short of it.* (*Merry Wives of Windsor* Act 2 Scene 2).

The journalist and author Bernard Levin once wrote a humorous piece quoting many lines from Shakespeare which are used in our everyday speech. It is available on a poster from the Globe Theatre – http://www.shakespearesglobe.com/shop/product/quoting-shakespeare-poster/87. But language is constantly developing new means of communication and this can be seen in changes to writing style. Since Shakespeare's time, we've all read *lots* of other things, and we've absorbed *them* into our collective literary consciousness.

If you read widely, you will increase your vocabulary, notice many different ways in which you can structure your writing, and you'll have access to the best resource of all: a wealth of ideas. There's no copyright on ideas!

Finding your voice

Nobody writes in quite the same way as you do. So, the moment your pen touches the paper or your fingertip presses a key, something wonderful might happen. You could find you start to write creatively using your own unique voice.

If you then realise you've written something like *the cat sat on the mat,* however, it's likely this has come from your *memory.* A creative writing teacher will focus on helping you to tap into your *creativity.* You can access this creative source in a variety of ways, and one of the best is to write every day.

But – to write what? Well...try shutting your eyes, turning your head in another direction, opening your eyes and writing about what you can see. Or close your eyes, listen, open your eyes again and write about what you heard. Or write about what you had for lunch, the last shop you visited or a walk you took. Write about what is bothering or upsetting you or write about what makes you happy.

Write freely and, at this early stage, don't allow your internal editor to comment on your work. Keep going and always write a few lines beyond the point at which you first thought of stopping. Change the subject, change it back, write without worrying about making mistakes. Make notes instead of sentences if you can't get your thoughts down fast enough. Don't worry if your spelling isn't all that grate (*sic*). In fact, don't worry if what you write makes no sense at all.

How on earth can this be a good plan? Nobody will publish an incomprehensible story full of mistakes. It is unlikely to win a competition. But...

...every field of human endeavour, whether it's sculpting, gardening or writing a cracking good story, requires a coming-together of both *ideas* and *craft*. We learn some elements of the *craft* of writing at school. If we're to pass our exams, it's essential we get to grips with good writing practice – that we get our heads round conventional grammar, spelling and punctuation. Commercial publishers certainly expect us to get our basic presentation right.

But sometimes we are so afraid to break the rules that our imaginations are stifled. Free-writing as it is sometimes called, allows us to break all those rules. Who knows what we might find outside their confines? Some interesting ideas, perhaps?

After you've allowed your imagination free rein for a while, and have accumulated lots of ideas, you'll need to think about how you can put all this material into a story. We all organise our writing into sentences and paragraphs, but it is the *order* of our *ideas* that makes for a good story. So this is where the *craft* of writing comes back into play.

But where can you find these ideas?

If you're stuck for ideas, these can certainly be generated by reading the work of other writers. Reorganised, polished and newly-presented, these ideas might end up making good stories. Authors of fan fiction and of modernisations and/or continuations of existing stories are inspired by the work of other writers. The award-winning *Nice Work* by David Lodge is a very successful reworking of *North and South* by Elizabeth Gaskell. There are literally hundreds, if not thousands, of published and unpublished novels based on Jane Austen's characters – what happened to them next, what became of their children, how these characters might behave if they were alive today...

But what about new ideas? The ones that pop into your head from nowhere? How do you sort the good ones from the bad? If you write every day, you'll find you start to see what might work and what definitely won't. Writing down everything that comes into your head and covering ten or twenty sheets of A4 paper might seem labour-intensive and also very wasteful. But, when you're panning for gold, an awful lot of mud and gravel is likely to get shifted!

Don't leave home without a notebook or your phone. Often, ideas will pop into your head at inconvenient times and you'll need to write them down because otherwise they might vanish forever. This is especially true of those brilliant ideas which come to you while you're half asleep, dozing off or waking up. Leave yourself messages on voicemail, on your landline's answering machine, or record voice memos.

Take photographs that illustrate what you're thinking about right now – photographs not only of places but also of objects you come across which might be relevant to your story. As you're passing shop windows, maybe take snaps of clothes your characters might wear.

Listen to conversations and people-watch. Write a journal, a diary about what's happening to you and in the wider world. Have opinions about things. What would it be like to have *other* opinions? Imagine what it is like to be someone else. Imagine being *lots* of other people.

A creative writing teacher can encourage the writer within you. When you start to *think* like a writer, your unique writing voice will become all the clearer.

Helping you to improve

Hardly anybody actually *likes* criticism. So, although some people will agree their writing is probably all the better for it, others will stop writing at the first hint of anything less than adulation.

But only an irresponsible and dishonest teacher would praise anything and everything. An effective teacher will instil confidence in the novice writer by pointing out what is good about his or her writing rather than by dwelling on what is bad. This approach will provide the student with a much-needed defence against despair and disenchantment for times when the going gets really tough.

Students usually learn good practice by reading and analysing examples of successful writing, then by working through practical exercises on specific issues, such as characterisation or dialogue. Sometimes, the exercises a teacher sets may not seem relevant to the sort of writing you want to do. But nothing is lost by having a go at them. Often, the results can not only give you a pleasant surprise but also reveal an unsuspected talent.

You've written what you feel is a good story and are very proud of yourself. You take it along to a class or to your writing group, read it out and gradually the horrible truth dawns – everyone hated it. Or perhaps they didn't understand it, were bored or felt misled in some way. Of course, you might have written a masterpiece so brilliant and so far ahead of its time that everyone else is floundering. This could be so! But, all the same, you need to allow other people access to your work if only to steel yourself against those who tell you your writing is bad, you're wasting your time and not to bother.

Achieving what you set out to do is the measure of success. If you wish to write a passage in free-writing mode, as suggested in the section above, and you do it, that's fine. Pat yourself on the back. But if you write what you think is a perfect crime story which turns out to be so perfect that even you can't solve the crime, then you *haven't* succeeded.

As you begin your writing career, try to enjoy what you do. Aim to write for the sheer *pleasure* of writing. If your only goal is to write a bestseller and make a fortune, you might spend much or all of your life being miserable, especially if you don't really enjoy the writing process. When are you happier – while you are actually writing or when you stop writing and can have some time off? All writers need to take breaks, but they also need to enjoy the writing process, even if this is sometimes a rather masochistic pleasure.

Most of us need another pair of eyes to see *between* the lines we've written. Critiquing our own work can be akin to looking at ourselves in the mirror but with our noses pressed up against the glass. Yes, we can see, but not very well. Putting a story to one side and looking at it again some time in the future can be helpful when it comes to spotting flaws. But discussing the story with an astute and experienced teacher can be a quicker and more productive process.

Information

You should expect your teacher to know about the *craft* of writing. We'll talk more about this in Chapter 2, but for now…

In a class or group situation you can learn a great deal by listening to other people reading their work aloud and by sharing your own writing with your peers. But, if you wish to take your writing further, submit it to a literary agent or publisher, or perhaps enter competitions, advice from someone who is a little (or a lot) further along the writing road will probably be of most benefit. A teacher or one-to-one mentor, with whom you connect face-to-face or find online, will be able to follow your progress closely and tailor his or her comments to what you are writing. But you will need to find someone you can trust and who understands your work. Be clear about what you want to achieve, then your mentor will be able to help you get there.

As is the case with most things human beings do, the more you know, the more you will realise how much there is still to know. One of the many joys of writing is that there is no end to experimentation, invention and possibility.

At any level above beginners, and definitely at university level, you should receive guidance about where and how to submit your work if it's to have the best chance of commercial or competition success. If you wish to publish your own work either in hard copy or online, we advise you to seek editorial help before going ahead.

Don't be told but do listen to reason

You can write about whatever you like.

But, as a writer, you are a communicator. So you need to respect those with whom you are communicating – or trying to communicate. Some students wonder why their short stories have been rejected or don't win competitions, but further investigation reveals they neither read nor like the genre in which they chose to write that story.

Writing in various styles and in different genres, done in a spirit of exploration and learning, is all to the good. If, however, a teacher suggests you should write a romantic novel about a wannabe fashion designer in the nineteen-fifties, when you'd thought of writing about the first human settlement on Mars, ask your teacher why the suggestion was made.

It will probably be based on the teacher's observation of where your writing strengths lie. Perhaps all the struggle you had with the Mars colony will drop away when you dress your heroine in bobby socks and the furthest distance she wishes to travel is into town on a Saturday night.

If you write frequently – if you keep journals, write reams of stream-of-consciousness material or structured short stories, flash fiction or novels, and you keep all this as hard copy – it won't be

very long before you start wondering whether to
buy more shelves!

Who are you?

As a writer, who are you? Do you have your own
distinctive writing voice? If you've never looked
through your body of accumulated work, it
might be worth checking it out in case you are
missing something important about your writing.
Is there a subject to which you keep returning? Is
your writing fantasy-oriented or is it rooted in
fact? Or both? Do relationships matter? Romance
or Family? Crime or Comedy? Is your style
conversational or rather formal? Do you write
verse but are you reluctant to call yourself a poet?
Do you have a wide vocabulary? Is your writing
suitable for children or young adults rather than
over-eighteens?

Among these pages you might find lots of good
ideas you have forgotten, surprising insights
about yourself and perhaps a clear way forward
for your writing.

Nobody but you

It's a fact that even the best creative writing teachers in the world cannot make you into a great writer if the potential isn't there. They may offer advice and guidance, but they cannot do the actual writing for you.

Fortunately, the writing world has always been wide, and these days it's even wider because the world has come into every home in the shape of an oblong screen. Writing which does not make it into high street bookshops through the usual channels can be made available to the reading public on screen. Life writing, blogs, erotica, fan fiction, commentary, non-fiction: it's all out there on the net. Millions of people everywhere are tapping on keyboards and making it happen.

No guarantees

You have a master's degree in creative writing. Your tutor loves your story. So does your mother and your husband or wife. In fact, everyone you know loves your story. They've never read better. You choose your competition carefully. Yes, you've read the rules, sent it in before the closing date and paid your fee.

You don't win. Or come second or third. How can that be?

You've redrafted your novel four times. It's taken you eighteen months. Your mentor is happy. You send it for a professional critique which comes back saying that with a few minor revisions it will be wonderful. It wins a prize. A literary agent likes your first three chapters and wants to read it all. She takes you on. You have an agent and you dare to dream. The agent doesn't sell your book. Publishers love it but say they don't know how to market it. It's not what they're looking for right now. Last year, yes. Not now: too dated.

Both the examples above are everyday occurrences for writers. We live in a subjective world. The infinite number of ways in which words can be put together to produce all the myriad stories there are in the world is a source of wonder. But getting those words in front of millions of appreciative readers is often down to luck, to a fluke, to chance.

It's easy for us to say this, but – never give up. You can't always arrange for luck to come your way, but you can try to make things happen for you by going to writers' conferences and festivals, by meeting people who might help you, by learning about the publishing process and by talking to industry professionals in a relaxed, informal setting. So keep writing, because nobody can publish what you haven't yet written!

Life saving

Creative writing can be very therapeutic but a creative writing teacher is not a therapist.

A creative writing student will often be given this advice – write what you know. But what *do* you know? It's a colossal question. There is immediate information: we know about ourselves, our feelings and relationships. We know about our surroundings and the experiences which we keep in our memories. We also have acquired knowledge – for example, we know there are distant galaxies and that in 1066 William of Normandy came and conquered England. We have so much knowledge that we can see into the future, too. I shall visit my friend tomorrow. The weather forecast is stormy and I must remember to take my umbrella when I go out. Already I am constructing the story of my tomorrow.

Your own personal experience is the most vivid to you and is full of the kind of detail that can help to bring your writing to life. But our lives are sometimes painful or unhappy and recalling certain events in them can be distressing. When this distress is reflected back to us on the page, in our free-writing or through the mouths of our characters, it can be very shocking, so a measure of distance or detachment might be required. Often, when we are writing about our own experiences, a sense of humour is definitely desirable.

But aren't you writing fiction? What if you are writing a novel set in the tenth century or that one about the first colony on Mars? You can imagine the surface of Mars and it will probably be nothing like the real thing. But it will do, and you can explore as you go along, much as those first colonists did.

If your book is about imaginary Martians, rather than humans, you can make *them* up too, but always bear in mind that it is the complexity of humans, their intellects and emotions, likes, dislikes, ambitions and fears, all their myriad foibles and the lives they lead that make characters in fiction interesting. If we're to believe novelists and film makers, it seems a great many aliens share human characteristics. Perhaps they might be missing the more benign of our qualities, and their greed and aggression might make them terrifying. Or perhaps, like E T, they share our good points, and we are charmed.

Writers need to know about humans. Like actors, we create lots of different characters, so imagining what it is like to be someone else is part of our job. We both are and are not our characters. You might have invented a villain who is the vilest murderer who ever lived, but this doesn't mean you are a wicked and depraved person yourself.

The imagination conjures up the good, the bad, the hideous and the beautiful.

Exercise

Close your eyes and think of a room that is very familiar to you. Try to see it in your mind's eye. It could be your home or place of work or maybe

somewhere you remember from your childhood.
Think of what you like and dislike, what you
value about it. Don't get too involved in what
may have happened in this room. Look, listen,
pick things up if you like. Run your finger tips
over the surfaces.

Open your eyes and write a paragraph or two
about the room.

Now imagine you are one of the following three
people:

1 - A burglar
2 - An old acquaintance you haven't seen for
years
3 - A small child

Then write about the room again, this time
through his or her eyes.

CHAPTER 2

The craft of creative writing

What is a story?
Character or Plot?
Character
Plot
Narrative Viewpoint
Dialogue

We are creative writers, so we write stories.

But what is a story, and what does it need to do?

A story is a description of human behaviour, and this behaviour needs to have consequences – in other words, it needs to have a plot.

The story must introduce the reader to a person or people (or to animal(s) or robot(s) or toy(s) or alien(s) standing in for people) who

want something, and
try to get this something, and
make some kind of physical and/or emotional and/or moral journey.

In a story

actions have results, and
characters make choices which determine what happens next, and
all (or most of) the questions which are asked at the beginning of the story are answered at the end.

If you're writing a series of interlinked stories or novels, you can sometimes leave one or two questions unanswered, as Janet Evanovich does in her Stephanie Plum stories – will Stephanie and Joe Morelli ever make up their minds about each other?

Something all story formats have in common is that they are (or they should be) about a character or characters who do things, make choices, meet challenges, come up against problems, who find themselves in conflict situations, and whose actions and choices affect what happens in the end.

When you're thinking about writing a story, you'll always need to ask yourself seven things:

1 - Whose story am I telling?
2 - What does this person (or what do these people) want?
3 - Who or what is going to help them to get what they want?
4 - Who or what is going to get in their way?
5 - What will go right?
6 - What will go wrong?
7 - What will happen in the end?

This may sound shocking. Surely it can't be true? Your favourite books reduced to providing the answers to **seven simple questions**?

But analysing your favourite books by asking and answering these seven questions will show you how a story works:

In J.R.R. Tolkien's *Lord of the Rings*:

1 - It's Frodo's story.
2 - He wants to destroy the One Ring (okay, he *must* rather than he *wants* to destroy it).
3 - The Fellowship, Elves, Dwarves etc. The good, particularly his friend Sam, help him.
4 - Orcs, Black Riders, Sauron's armies etc. The bad, particularly his adversary Gollum, hinder him.

5 - He reaches Mount Doom.
6 - He is wounded in all sorts of ways.
7 - He's successful but at a price – his wounds never really heal.

In Jane Austen's *Pride and Prejudice*:

1 - It's Elizabeth Bennet's story.
2 - She wants to marry a man she can respect, but if she doesn't marry Mr Collins her mother and sisters will lose their home on the day her father dies.
3 - Her strength of character and her father's backing help her to say *no* to the awful Mr Collins.
4 - Wealthy Mr Darcy proposes, but his pride prejudices him against her family. Elizabeth's pride is stung by his prejudice, plus she is seduced by Mr Wickham's lies which prejudice her against Mr Darcy.
5 - Both Mr Darcy and Elizabeth realise they have been wrong.
6 - Lydia's inappropriate behaviour threatens Elizabeth's and Mr Darcy's relationship. Lady Catherine de Bourgh seeks to forbid their marriage.
7 - Although they are confronted by all sorts of reasons why they *shouldn't* marry, the love between Elizabeth and Mr Darcy overcomes all obstacles.

You can see this structure in operation in even the simplest of nursery rhymes:

In *Incy Wincy Spider*:

1 - It's Incy's story.
2 - She wants to climb the waterspout.
3 - There's nobody to help – she's on her own here.
4 - The rain hinders her by washing her out.
5 – But, even though she's being discouraged by fate and circumstances, she has a strong character and she's still determined to climb the spout.
6 - The sun dries the rain.
7 - Success – Incy climbs the spout again. (This could go on for some time.)

Think about other stories you know and try to answer all the questions we've suggested above – *whose* story, *what* does he/she want, and so on. If it's not immediately obvious, don't give up. Unless you are thinking of something very experimental, you will find these specific questions are answered in all the stories you choose.

Once you've finished your novel, you'll have to write a synopsis or outline of it for a literary agent or publisher to see. Analysing how your story actually works will help you to write this synopsis. We'll talk about writing synopses later in the book.

Character or plot?

People who write stories are often asked: which do you think of first, your character(s) or your plot(s)? This is a bit like being asked: does day follow night, or does night follow day? When we set out to tell a story, we need a character or characters, and we need interesting situations in which these characters can act.

Some stories are predominantly *character-driven*, while others are predominantly *plot-driven*. But all kinds of stories need characters, and every story must describe some problematic or interesting situation, then show how this situation is ameliorated or resolved.

The classic worldwide bestseller *Catch 22* is predominantly *character-driven*. Although most of us want to know what happens to the American airman hero Yossarian – if he will be killed on a bombing mission or if he will manage to get himself grounded and out of the conflict – most readers find they are just as interested in the rest of the characters and their personal histories, even if these people are only tenuously linked to Yossarian.

The traditional fairy story *Cinderella* is predominantly *plot-driven*. We're not told much about Cinderella herself, so we have to make assumptions about where she lives, her age, her appearance, her likes and dislikes. We learn nothing about the hero except that he's a prince who falls in love with a stranger. This is acceptable because most of us already know all about fairytale princes and princesses, and because it's fine to encourage your reader to use his or her own imagination – to make Cinderella herself blonde or brunette or red-headed, and to make the prince traditionally handsome or maybe not. We read the story because we want to know what *happens* – if Cinderella escapes from her life of drudgery and marries the prince or maybe not.

Most jokes are plot-driven. A man walks into a pub, but it doesn't usually matter what he looks like, what he's wearing, or which pub. It's what happens next that's important. A man walks into a pub and he says or does what? This is the start of the story.

Your own story could take the form of a novel, a novella, a short story, a piece of flash fiction, a screenplay, a drama intended for film, television or radio performance, a comedy sketch, a narrative poem such as *Hiawatha* or *Paradise Lost*, or even a single joke.

Character

A story is always about a human being (or a rabbit, a machine, a fairy, a ghost or some other entity standing in for a human being) who wants or needs something, even if at first it's not apparent to the character or to the reader what this something might be.

It's usually possible to identify the parts played by different characters and to work out how they contribute to the development of the story.

Who is your hero or heroine?

For the purposes of this book, we shall refer to the main character of any story as the hero or heroine, even if their behaviour is not at all heroic. He or she is the **protagonist** – the person whose fate matters most, who wants something, and who hopes to get it. The heroes and heroines of romantic fiction want to find their soul mates.

The heroes and heroines of crime fiction want to solve crimes. If you take the hero or heroine out of your story, the story will not exist. The hero and heroine are the people with whom you'll want your reader to identify or even to fall in love. Or, if you're writing a savage farce about people who are all basically unpleasant, your hero and/or heroine will be the people about whom you'll want your reader to *care* or at least be *curious*. Tom Sharpe's classic satire *Blott on the Landscape* is a good example of a story in which everyone is fairly horrible, but most readers probably find they care about the fates of the hero and heroine, the ingenious gardener Blott and his beloved Lady Maude.

Your **villain** or **villainess**, who is sometimes called the **antagonist**, is there to stop the hero or heroine getting what he or she wants. It's often great fun to write about wicked people, but they shouldn't be more interesting than your heroes or heroines, or more sympathetic, and your reader shouldn't cry when they die. An attractive, clever, lazy bad guy can sometimes end up being much more fascinating and appealing – to both author and reader – than an honourable, decent, hardworking good guy. So when you're creating protagonists and antagonists you'll need to be careful. The bad guys mustn't overshadow the good guys or steal the show.

A story doesn't necessarily have to have a villain or villainess in it. The hero or heroine can be thwarted or challenged by circumstance(s), accident(s), coincidence, fate, his or her own personality, or even by a well-meaning character who doesn't intend to cause a disaster but who does so (or comes close to doing so) all the same. A good example of a well-intentioned saboteur is Donkey in the *Shrek* series of films. Donkey tries to do his best for his friend Shrek, but screws up all the time.

The hero or heroine should always be challenged by someone or something, even if the challenge comes from inside himself or herself – if, for example, he or she has to deal with fear, suspicion or pain of some kind. Will Traynor, the hero of Jojo Moyes's bestseller *Me Before You*, is challenged by his own determination to put a stop to all the stuff that's messing up his difficult life and also by his growing affection for the heroine, Louisa. If your hero or heroine isn't challenged, you won't have much of a story.

Your major characters will sometimes need to have **friends**, **enemies**, **mentors**, **guides**, **confidantes** and **facilitators** – people who will help or hinder them as they try to get what they want.

Suspense, crime and mystery stories often introduce the reader to characters who might be good guys or bad guys – people who seem well-disposed towards the hero and/or heroine, but who might be working towards their destruction. In Daphne du Maurier's *Rebecca*, for example, the grief-stricken housekeeper Mrs Danvers is working towards the heroine's destruction from Day One, but it takes the heroine a long time to work that out.

You can always let your reader wonder about your characters, at least at the beginning of the story. A bad guy doesn't need to be hideous or have cloven hooves. A good guy doesn't need to be physically gorgeous or have angel's wings. A little or even a lot of complexity of character is always a good thing.

Hero, heroine, villain, villainess, friend, enemy, mentor, guide, confidante, facilitator, man or woman of mystery who might be a friend or a foe – whenever you read a story yourself, try to identify which roles the various characters are playing. Then, when you write your own fiction, give your characters specific parts to play.

Plot

If a character goes to town, does her shopping, comes home again and puts her feet up with a welcome mug of coffee, all that won't add up to a plot. This is because unless she spills her coffee down her best frock and/or ruins her new carpet and/or scalds her foot and needs to go to A&E where she meets a gorgeous doctor and falls in love or gets kidnapped by the taxi driver taking her to hospital, there are unlikely to be any consequences.

But if she goes to town and meets someone she hasn't seen for years – someone who knows something which your character would not want to be generally known, and which could ruin her life – you will have the genesis of a plot, because this scenario asks questions. It suggests the character will need to make some choices and is likely to be challenged in some way. It invites us to wonder what will happen next.

How do you start a story, how do you develop it, and how do you end it?

Openings, developments and endings

A good **opening** is one that asks questions to which the reader will want answers. Who killed the murder victim and how will this person be caught? Who will marry whom? Where is the Michelangelo drawing? You need to suggest your most important question as soon as possible, because doing this will get your reader interested, and also suggest why this reader should read or listen to your story.

So try to avoid starting any kind of story with any of the four following:

1 - A description of the scenery. Of course, it is possible to point to a host of classic novels which begin just like this. But the nineteenth century reader did not access the world in the way we do, through airline travel, photography and the computer, cinema and television screens. It is very unusual for a contemporary novel for adults to contain illustrations, but when Charles Dickens's novels were serialised they were

splendidly illustrated by George Cruikshank, probably because readers felt they wanted and needed illustrations to set the scene.

2 - A scene in which something happens that isn't actually going to matter. In *Pride and Prejudice* there is a scene in which the Bennet sisters walk to Meryton to buy ribbons. While there, they meet some army officers, including the charming Mr Wickham. If they'd bought their ribbons and gone home without meeting anyone, the scene would have no purpose in terms of moving the story forward.

3 - An overview of the main character's life history. It's possible that your hero's or heroine's schooldays might have some bearing on your plot. If this is indeed the case, consider filtering in this backstory at appropriate times, on a need-to-know basis, rather than telling the reader all about your character's schooldays right at the beginning of your novel and effectively putting off starting your actual story.

4 - *Once upon a time… It was a dark and stormy night… Tom/Jane opened his/her eyes and got out of bed… In a land far away…* These openings are clichés and so, if you want to use them, you will need to subvert, re-imagine or twist them in some original way.

As for **development** – while a reader reads your story, you'll need to retain this reader's interest. You could do that by revealing a secret, by introducing a new character whom you might have mentioned in passing earlier in the story, by letting your romantic hero or heroine be distracted by a new lover, or by letting your investigator start to follow a false trail.

A new objective for a central character is almost always a good thing. Your hero or heroine could resolve to win back a faithless lover. Your investigator could believe he/she knows the identity of the killer and arrest this person, but then someone else could be murdered, and the investigator will have to rethink the whole investigation.

This sort of forward progress will hopefully keep your reader reading.

But don't let the excitement peak too soon. Save your biggest drama or showdown for towards the end of the story.

The **ending** will answer all or most of the questions you asked at the beginning of your story and will hopefully leave your reader feeling satisfied rather than mystified, cheated or annoyed. A good story shouldn't merely hang a series of portraits on a narrative wall and invite the reader to look at them. Most readers hope to be shown how things work out for your characters. These readers want to leave your characters in the places where they want and/or deserve to be.

Does all this always have to be the case? Well, in a murder mystery the victim probably doesn't deserve to be dead. But if the story is to have any reader-appeal, you will probably need to bring the murderer to justice. You might know of one or two stories in which the killer gets away with it. But remember there are several million others in which he or she doesn't! The reason for this is that storytellers need to offer reader-satisfaction. If a killer gets away with murder, it makes for an unsatisfactory read. It feels wrong because murder is inherently wrong, and because most of us believe murderers should be caught and punished.

Do you always need to offer the reader a *happy* ending?

No, you definitely don't, even if you're writing *mainstream* (in *category* fiction published by Mills & Boon, a happy ending is obligatory) romantic fiction. But you *do* have to offer the reader the *right* ending, and it can be difficult to decide what the right ending should be.

Charles Dickens wrote two endings to *Great Expectations*, the second at the behest of his novelist friend Edward Bulwer Lytton. But, in this second ending, it's still not clear what really happened to Pip and Estella. *I saw no shadow of another parting from her* – what does *that* mean? Did Pip end up with Estella or not? Did they marry or did they part? Does it matter? Maybe not, because by the end of the novel Pip and Estella have reached a better understanding of each other, and this is what *really* needs to happen if the reader is to close the novel with a sigh of satisfaction.

Narrative viewpoint

You need to decide through whose eyes you want to see the action of your story. You'll probably have noticed already that in narrative formats like novels, the action is usually seen from the point(s) of view of one or more of the central characters. But which character(s) should you choose?

Most traditional stories are told from the point(s) of view of the hero and/or the heroine, in either the first or the third person. You don't have to do it this way, but you should bear in mind that if you write from the viewpoint of your bad guy, for example, the reader is likely to start identifying with him. You might not want this to happen. If you give a character a narrative viewpoint, he or she is likely to become the reader's friend. So choose your viewpoint character(s) carefully.

The first person viewpoint (*I did this, I said that*) is the most intimate, and it is often chosen by first time writers. Its main drawback is that it is difficult to let the reader know anything which the viewpoint character cannot or must not know. Also, if your viewpoint character isn't attractive or charismatic in some way, the reader is unlikely to become involved in your story.

Here are two examples of first person narrative viewpoint:

The first narrator is young Pip in *Great Expectations* by Charles Dickens:

The man, after looking at me for a moment, turned me upside down, and emptied my pockets. There was nothing in them but a piece of bread. When the church came to itself – for he was so sudden and strong that he made it go head over heels before me, and I saw the steeple under my feet – when the church came to itself, I say, I was seated on a high tombstone, trembling, while he ate the bread ravenously.

Here is Jane in Charlotte Brontë's *Jane Eyre*:

As I rose and dressed, I thought over what had happened, and wondered if it were a dream. I could not be certain of the reality till I had seen Mr Rochester again, and heard him renew his words of love and promise.

The reader is in these characters' heads, feeling what they feel – fear, panic, doubt, anxiety – and identifying with them completely.

The third person viewpoint (*he/she/it did this, he/she/it said that*) is much more flexible. If you wish, you can tell your whole story from the point(s) of view of the hero and/or heroine. Or you can tell just *some* of it from their point(s) of view and, when they are off the page, someone else can take over.

When you decide to write in the third person, you will have a big choice of viewpoint characters. But maybe you should restrict yourself to one or at most two in a short story, and up to about five or six in a novel, because otherwise you will find you are changing the narrative viewpoint all the time, and that your story will become disjointed. There will be far too many people trying to have their say, and your reader might get tired of listening to them.

Does the postman have to tell the reader what he feels about delivering letters on a wet winter day? Does the bus driver have to complain to the reader about the stroppy, rowdy passengers eating fish and chips on the top deck of his bus? If these characters and these events do not advance the action of your story, almost certainly not!

It's probably most engaging for the reader if you can write each scene in your story from just one or two characters' points of view, because otherwise you will end up head-hopping and your reader will be trying to listen to three or four or even more characters at the same time.

Here is an example of head-hopping:

Tom willed the lift to go faster. Suddenly, in its mirror-glass wall, he noticed a white patch of dried toothpaste on his chin, which he slapped at roughly. As soon as the doors opened wide enough for him to get through, he was running down the corridor.

Damn, thought Tom, when he saw everyone was already seated. I'm last. I wonder what they've been saying. I bet they think my spaceship is too expensive. He rubbed his chin again in case any toothpaste remained.

'Ah, there you are, Tom,' said Carol, wondering if he knew he had toothpaste on his chin. 'We're glad to see you.'

'This spaceship of yours looks promising,' said Steve, but as he spoke his mobile rang. 'Sorry,' he said, and went to take the call in the corridor. It was his wife…

We began with Tom, hopped into Carol's head when she thought about the toothpaste on Tom's chin, and then hopped into Steve's head, whereupon we left both Tom and Carol behind to go with Steve into the corridor.

When you write any scene, it's a good plan to imagine you are holding the hand of the character with whom you want your reader to engage throughout. In the above extract, we have to let go of Tom's hand, run round the table to see Tom through Carol's eyes, and then we follow Steve into the corridor. This sort of thing can be very effortful for readers!

When you do change the narrative viewpoint, you should normally indicate this by a line break. Then your reader will realise he/she is now in someone else's head.

Jane Austen's six major novels are all written in the third person, *almost entirely* from her heroines' points of view.

Here is Emma observing Frank Churchill and Harriet:

At first it was downright dullness to Emma. She had never seen Frank Churchill so silent and stupid. He said nothing worth hearing – looked without seeing – admired without intelligence – listened without knowing what she said. While he was so dull, it was no wonder that Harriet should be dull likewise, and they were both insufferable.

Jane Austen *Emma*

But Anthony Trollope writes in the third person from *several* points of view:

Eleanor was herself the widow of a medical man, and felt a little inclined to resent all these hard sayings. But Miss Thorne was so essentially good-natured that it was impossible to resent anything she said. Eleanor therefore sipped her wine and finished her chicken.

Mr Harding winced at the idea of the press. He had had enough of that sort of publicity, and was unwilling to be shown up a second time either as a monster or as a martyr.

Mr Arabin looked at her piteously. It seemed to him as though he were being interrogated by some inner spirit of his own, to whom he could not refuse an answer, and to whom he did not dare give a false reply.

Anthony Trollope *Barchester Towers*

It's possible to combine the advantages of the first and third person points of view by writing in the deep third person. What is **deep third person viewpoint**? It's a style of writing which takes the reader deep inside the head (and heart and soul) of the character in the way a first person narrative viewpoint does extremely effectively, but which also allows for the multi-viewpoint flexibility of a third person narrative.

A passage written in deep third person narrative viewpoint looks like this:

What the hell did he think he was playing at?
Madeleine checked the screen one more time. Yes, there was the text. She hadn't imagined it.
Bastard.
She'd give him hell when he came home. Shame he'd forgotten his BlackBerry that morning.
Shame for Jack, anyway.

If you look at the example above again, you will see that it could easily be reworked as a first person narrative because it is so intensely focused – the reader is invited to *become* the character as he or she reads the story. A traditional, classical, more detached third person narrative might not be quite so immediately involving for the reader, especially if the author has a voice himself or herself – if the author butts in, as some authors do, and writes things like *Madeleine was very angry with Jack.*

A deep third person narrative perspective tends not to need so many speech tags or indications of who is speaking because this is usually perfectly obvious.

Nowadays, many novelists write in the deep third person in order to make sure they dig that little bit – well – deeper! You can find more notes on deep third person narrative viewpoint on this link: http://theeditorsblog.net/2011/11/16/deep-pov-whats-so-deep-about-it/

What about the second person narrative voice, in which the reader is told *you did this* or *you said that*? In some cases, *you* means *I*, the narrator, and this often seems to be a literary affectation. If you mean *I*, why should you write *you*? Or it can mean *you, the reader*, and this can sound somewhat accusatory.

There are some notes on second person narratives on this link – http://tvtropes.org/pmwiki/pmwiki.php/Main/SecondPersonNarration. If you're a first time novelist aspiring to commercial publication, we don't suggest you go for this narrative option unless you feel very strongly that you have no choice.

It's also possible to tell stories from the perspective of the all-seeing author or God, and sometimes Anthony Trollope does – he writes from his characters' narrative viewpoints and also from his own. This eye-of-God method of storytelling is not hugely popular with readers nowadays, and it sometimes tends to result in a rather detached, matter-of-fact story. The author manipulates the characters, and the reader can often see the strings, whereas in an ideal world the reader of a novel should forget about the author and connect with the characters one-to-one.

But, if you *want* to write from your own authorial point of view, there's nothing to stop you, and you will be able to find examples of this approach in both classic and contemporary fiction. If the author has a particularly attractive voice, this approach to story-telling can work very well. William Makepeace Thackeray wrote *Vanity Fair* from his own authorial viewpoint, and the American novelist Fannie Flagg often makes her own voice heard.

Lastly, we should mention the narrative viewpoint of the sympathetic (or sometimes unsympathetic or downright hostile) observer, a person who is not directly involved with the fates of the protagonist(s) in a story, but who is instead looking on and taking notes for the reader.

The tenant Mr Lockwood and the servant Mrs Dean are the narrative voices in **Emily Brontë's** *Wuthering Heights*, a story in which the central characters are not particularly attractive, have a rather bad time and end up being the architects of their own destruction. But the two narrators are very ordinary. They are people like us. Perhaps it's easier to identify with people like us? What do you think?

Dialogue

You've created your characters, you've given them a drama in which to act, you've decided who is going to have a narrative viewpoint, so now let's hear these characters talking.

What does effective dialogue do?

It reveals personality, it takes the action forward, and it helps the reader to connect with the characters. It allows this reader to forget the story is all invention, and he or she needn't believe a word of it.

As we read a story, most of us want to believe!

If you look at the following two examples, you will be able to decide which style of storytelling works more effectively.

Example 1:

She told him it was all over and she wanted to split up. He was very upset and wanted to know why.

Example 2:

'It's all over,' she said. 'I think it would be best if we split up.'

'But why?' he demanded, staring at her in disbelief. 'What's gone wrong? What have I done?'

'You haven't done anything. It's not you, it's me. My feelings have changed, all right?'

'I know you're having a bad time at work,' he said, and reached out to touch her hand. 'You want to leave this town and do something new. I can't say I blame you. But surely you don't have to throw everything away?'

'I told you, it's over!' she snapped, and shook him off. 'What don't you understand?'

'There's someone else, isn't there?'

'No,' she said, and turned away from him.

'Then it must be about me, and I'm entitled to an explanation.'

'I can't give you one.'

If you read that second passage aloud, you'll be able to hear the different tones of voice, which in turn express the characters' personalities, feelings and states of mind.

She is determined to take a specific course of action. Perhaps she is afraid he's going to try to stop her leaving. So she ends up being mean to him, probably because she's scared that if she tries to be kind he'll talk her out of going, and she doesn't want to give him the chance. She's behaving like a trapped insect. She's desperate to escape, and she doesn't care if she hurts herself or anyone else in the process.

He is puzzled, upset, and at first he tries to empathise with her feelings. But then – because we all like to understand how we have upset someone, and why they are offended – he becomes suspicious, and determined to have an explanation.

She is equally determined not to give him one. But the fact that she turns away when she tells him no one else is involved will make him and the reader suspect she is having an affair.

The author hasn't had to explain to the reader that these two characters are anxious, worried, bewildered, determined, mean, sympathetic or suspicious, because it's all there in the dialogue.

Look at this section of dialogue:

'You're telling me you're afraid?'

'I'm terrified.' Alex looked at Rose. 'I didn't use to be. I thought the men who shirked and cried were cowards, who should be put against the wall. But that was in another life, before I dared to hope. Rose, when I had no hope, I had no fear.'

'I know it must be horrible.' Rose took his hand and stroked the scarred, bruised knuckles. 'I know I would be scared.'

'Rose, you don't understand. I'm not exactly scared – most of the time I just get on with it. Sometimes I enjoy it.'

'Do you?'

'Yes, because it's all a game, and I'm quite good at it. But soldiers are supposed to fight, and what we're doing these days isn't fighting.'

'What is it, then?'

'We're murdering each other, and it's not the same.'

Margaret James *The Silver Locket*

Do you see all that white space? Does it make the page look welcoming and reader-friendly? Big blocks of narrative and long paragraphs can be very off-putting, encouraging the reader to skip or skim. But lots of white space on a page somehow makes it seem accessible and inviting.

Dialogue tends to be written in short paragraphs, is intimate and confiding, and readers are far more likely to remember what they've read in dialogue because, even after they have finished reading the story, they will hear the voices of the characters inside their heads.

It's worth thinking about *how* your characters speak because otherwise there's a danger they will *all* sound like you (or perhaps like people you know or have heard on the radio or television). This could be unfortunate because it's unlikely you will want your characters to sound like the Queen or the man in the newsagent's shop.

If you are writing about a tiny island community which has had no outside influences for several generations and, as a result, everyone uses the same vocabulary and phraseology, there's a possibility the reader will have difficulty distinguishing between the people in your story. But, even in such an extreme situation, your characters should probably have their own recognisable voices, and you should be able to find ways to make their speech patterns and diction individual.

Novelists need to be able to pick up the patterns and rhythms of real dialogue and to reproduce these patterns and rhythms in their writing. But, when you're writing dialogue, you don't need to include every single word you'd probably hear in a real conversation. In everyday speech, common expressions such as *to be honest* or *know what I mean*, and words like *well* and *anyway* litter our conversations, but we don't tend to hear them. On the page, however, they draw attention to themselves. So don't overuse them.

Here are the four main influences on the way we speak:

1 - Age
2 - Geographical locality
3 - Social class
4 - Peer group

Every group of people has its own vocabulary, use of expression, manner and jargon. There is no substitute for keeping your ears open and listening, not only to *what* people say, but *how* they say it.

Imagine you have been introduced to someone new and you are telling a friend all about him. Would you say:

He's a nice chap or *he's a good bloke* or maybe *he's a cool dude*? Perhaps you would say he's a *guy*, a *nerd*, a *plank* or a *dork*, or maybe an *altogether spiffing fellow*?

Perhaps *you* wouldn't say any of the above – but a character might. Each term or expression comes with its own connotations which the reader will then interpret in order to learn more about the speaker.

Character, **plot**, **narrative viewpoint** and **dialogue** – if you use these effectively you will end up with good stories.

Exercise

Think of someone you know, or from the media, and then make a short list of attributes which you associate with this person.

Perhaps these could include a job, an item of clothing, a favourite place, a mannerism and a hobby? The list could be longer if you like, but you'll need to repeat the exercise by making a list for three, four or five different people.

Randomly choose attributes from each list and imagine a composite character. Write a paragraph about this character in a few fairly commonplace situations. Shopping, in a waiting room, at a party, perhaps? How do they behave? Are they shy or confident? Patient or pushy? Funny or boorish?

How do they speak? What interests them? Can you look at the world through their eyes? Would you like to talk to them at that party or would you avoid them?

Are they somebody a reader might be interested in? If not, why not?

Exercise

Look at the paragraph below. It's the opening of *Middlemarch* by **George Eliot**. It introduces us to Miss Dorothea Brooke and her sister, Celia.

What is your reaction to how it looks on the page?

Read the passage through and write a couple of scenarios in which these two sisters (or two other sisters) might be introduced in a *contemporary* novel. Storytelling techniques, style and diction – who would write *thrown into relief by poor dress* nowadays? – have changed a lot since this novel was first published in 1874.

Miss Brooke had that kind of beauty which seems to be thrown into relief by poor dress. Her hand and wrist were so finely formed that she could wear sleeves not less bare of style than those in which the Blessed Virgin appeared to Italian painters; and her profile as well as her stature and bearing seemed to gain the more dignity from her plain garments, which by the side of provincial fashion gave her the impressiveness of a fine quotation from the Bible, - or from one of our elder poets, - in a paragraph of to-day's newspaper. She was usually spoken of as being remarkably clever, but with the addition that her sister Celia had more common-sense. Nevertheless, Celia wore scarcely more trimmings; and it was only to close observers that her dress differed from her sister's, and had a shade of coquetry in its arrangements; for Miss Brooke's plain dressing was due to mixed conditions, in most of which her sister shared. The pride of being ladies had something to do with it: the Brooke connections, though not exactly aristocratic, were unquestionably "good:" if you inquired backward for a generation or two, you would not find any yard-measuring or parcel-tying forefathers - anything lower than an admiral or a clergyman; and there was even an ancestor discernible as a Puritan gentleman who served under Cromwell, but afterwards conformed, and managed to come out of all political troubles as the proprietor of a respectable family estate.

CHAPTER 3

Building Your Story

How is it for you?
Questions your reader will ask
When, where and how to start
Maintaining tension
Words

This chapter will discuss these important subjects in detail.

How is it for you?

There are many ways in which you can build a story, and sometimes it's hard to find the one that's right for you.

When you're first thinking about a story:

1 - you could write a detailed plan or synopsis and stick to it, or

---

2 - you could write a vague outline and be prepared to change it, or
3 - you could do no planning at all and hope your characters will show you the way.

What are the advantages and disadvantages of these three working methods?

Once the **planners** have their plans in place, they tend to feel relieved. Now, they'll always know where they are going, so they'll rarely suffer from panic attacks, and they're unlikely to get blocked. But they'll also risk losing interest in their stories because they'll know exactly what happens before they write a single word of the stories themselves.

The **vague outliners** have the security of a road map, but they'll wait until they start writing the actual story before they finalise the details of their characters' journeys. They're not likely to become bored because they'll always be willing to let their characters surprise them. They'll be happy to change their original plans if they think of something better or more interesting for their characters to do. They might panic once in a while because they don't always know what to write next. But, if this should happen, they know they can always write a few key scenes which come later in the story, and then join the dots or build a bridge over the ravine!

The **planning phobics** often say planning stifles their creativity. They fear that planning a story in detail might make their writing seem leaden and dull. But authors who don't plan anything are also at risk of writing themselves into dead ends or of getting depressed when they find a story line isn't developing as well as they'd hoped. Sometimes, when they are several thousand words into a story, they realise they don't actually like their characters and/or they really don't know what to do with these people. They often spend their precious writing hours fretting or staring out of the window because they don't know what to write today. So they tend to waste a lot of time. They're the ones who are most likely to write the first three chapters of a novel or to start a short story with huge enthusiasm, but then to run out of steam and inspiration.

Most commercially-published novelists have to be planners, at least to some extent, because if they are under contract to publishers they usually have to keep their editors informed about any current work-in-progress and/or to let these editors have outlines or short synopses of what they intend to write next. *What are you writing now* and *what are you going to write next* – professional novelists are asked these questions all the time.

When you write your stories, do you tend to over-write or under-write?

Almost all of us do one or the other!

Some authors deliberately over-write, putting in absolutely everything they think might have a place in their stories. This is fine as long as they are aware that some of this material – episodes which are complete in themselves, perhaps, and don't contribute anything to the great scheme of things, or characters who appear and later disappear without doing anything to advance the action – will end up being redundant and will need to come out.

Other authors begin with notes and sketches. They gradually build their stories from the inside out, adding to their word counts day by day, and always aware of how much they have yet to do. This approach can make for good time management because they hardly ever have to cut anything – everything they write will be there for a purpose. It will reveal character and/or it will move the story on.

Planner, vague outliner or planning phobic, over-writer or under-writer, here are some guidelines which should help you to write a better story.

When, where and how will you start?

A good place to begin could be when your hero and/or heroine:

1 - needs to make a choice, or
2 - is presented with a challenge, or
3 - meets the person who is going to change his or her life, or
4 - changes his or her status – marries, is widowed, become a parent, is orphaned, is abandoned by a husband, wife or lover, leaves school, leaves home, starts a new job, retires from a profession, or
5 - must deal with a setback of some kind – is injured in battle, is bankrupted, is attacked, is bereaved, is made homeless, or
6 - makes an important decision, or
7 - makes a mistake.

As a result of any or all of the seven situations above, your hero and/or heroine will need to *do* something, and this need to act will give you a foundation on which to build your story. It will get your reader asking questions, which the reader will wish to do.

Questions your reader may ask

Some good questions include:

1 - Who killed whom?
2 - Why and when and how did someone die?
3 - Who will marry or end up with whom?
4 - How will a beleaguered, wounded, frightened or unjustly imprisoned hero or heroine fight back?
5 - What happened to the money/baby/locket?

Where's it happening?

You've dreamed up your characters, you've given them choices and/or challenges, and now you need to think about your set-up.

Where and when is your story taking place? In what situation(s) do your characters find themselves when your action begins?

You're not writing a history book or a travel guide. So you'll need to suggest your set-up, which can include giving your reader some information about the physical setting of your story – past, present, town, countryside, East, West – without going into huge geographical or circumstantial detail.

One easy and painless way for you to describe your set-up and for your reader to understand what is going on at the start of your story is to let your characters talk about it.

Why should they talk about it?

Dialogue is always more reader-friendly than narrative. Direct speech wakes a story up, whereas long stretches of narrative tend to put it to sleep. When you're reading a novel or any other kind of story yourself, which do you find more appealing and engaging – dialogue or narrative? We're prepared to bet it's dialogue.

If you describe a set-up and/or setting in dialogue, as one character shows a scene to a second character, or as they both arrive somewhere new and talk about what they see, or as they discuss a problematic situation, the reader is likely to remember it.

You'll also need to ask yourself where your characters would like and/or deserve to be at the end of your story. If you're having trouble getting started, knowing where you want to go and working towards this might be a way forward for you.

But, if you can't envisage the ending yet, don't worry – work towards the middle of your story, towards a turning point or a new challenge for your hero or heroine. Perhaps he or she could have a flash of intuition, inspiration or enlightenment? When you get to that point, your hero or heroine could then decide what to do with this enlightenment, inspiration or intuition.

Perhaps the mistress nobody knew existed turns up at the funeral of her married lover? Perhaps a child dies? Perhaps a woman who believed she could never have children becomes pregnant? Perhaps a husband tells his wife he is gay and is leaving the family home? Perhaps…perhaps…

Maintaining tension

As you write, try to maintain tension and reader-interest by leaving your characters in difficult or interesting situations before moving on to a new set of circumstances or characters, rather than by turning out bedroom lights and letting these characters (and probably your reader, too) fall peacefully asleep.

Do you know the story of Scheherazade from *Tales of the Arabian Nights*?

She was ordered to tell her husband, who happened to be the Sultan, a story. Once the story was finished, she would be put to death. But, unlike many brides before her, Scheherazade realised that if she stopped at an exciting moment and promised to tell the rest of story the next day, she might keep her head a little longer. Eventually, the Sultan was so taken with her story that she kept her head for good.

When you write each chapter of your own novel or scene in your short story, it might be worth bearing the following maxim in mind: *begin with intrigue, end with jeopardy.*

Both intrigue and jeopardy come in subtle shades. Intrigue isn't necessarily of Byzantine complexity and jeopardy isn't always life threatening. All they need to do is tempt your reader to turn the page.

You will need to suit your pace to your story.

A crime or mystery story usually needs to be fast-paced because, if events move too slowly, the reader might solve the crime before the hero or heroine does. But fast-paced doesn't mean rushed, confusing or breathless. You'll need to strike a balance between keeping the story moving, keeping the reader guessing, and giving the reader *time* to guess – but not too much time! You'll also need to develop your central characters so that the reader will care about these people and want to know what happens to them.

Kate Atkinson's Jackson Brodie series of novels, which began with *Case Histories*, are great examples of fast-paced, exciting stories in which there is plenty of character-development. Readers of crime novels tend to love series and to become attached to the central characters in them. P D James's Dalgliesh and Colin Dexter's Morse have their own fan bases, as does Ruth Rendell's Wexford. So, even though most crime and mystery novels are plot-driven and need to be fast-paced, they need to introduce the reader to well-rounded central characters, too.

A traditional romantic story in which the hero and heroine are eventually going to find themselves happily united can be more leisurely in pace. But you'll still need to keep the tension tight and to give the reader some surprises. Since the reader will already know the hero and heroine must end up together, discovering *how* they find their happy-ever-after is what will keep this reader reading.

Try not to allow your characters to chat aimlessly – instead, always let their dialogue move the story on in some way and tell the reader (or even your characters themselves) something he or she doesn't already know about your characters' personalities and/or motivation.

If you tell your readers anything they *don't* need to know, you'll risk confusing them and making them wonder if they need to remember all this – or not? Dialogue in fiction should not be as discursive and casual as chatting in daily life. It must earn its place in your story, as Jane Austen pointed out to a young fan who sent the great novelist a story of her own:

The scene with Mrs Mellish, I should condemn; it is prosy and nothing to the purpose.

Jane Austen *Selected Letters*

If dialogue is *prosy* (is just casual chatting) and *nothing to the purpose* (doesn't move the action forward or tell the reader anything he/she needs to know), it definitely needs to come out – to be literally *condemned*.

Jane Austen gets it absolutely right herself in the piece of dialogue we've quoted below, which reveals character and moves the story on in a *small* but *very significant* way.

'Oh! Very well,' exclaimed Miss Bates, 'then I need not be uneasy. "Three things very dull indeed." That will just do for me, you know. I shall be sure to say three dull things as soon as ever I open my mouth, shan't I? – (looking round with the most good-humoured dependence on everyone's assent) – Do you not all think I shall?'

Emma could not resist.

'Ah! Ma'am, but there may be a difficulty. Pardon me – but you will be limited as to number – only three at once.'

Jane Austen *Emma*

Emma is suddenly made aware that she – the beautiful, talented, rich and gracious Miss Woodhouse, to whom the whole district must defer – can be pointlessly spiteful and cruel. This comes as a very unwelcome or even shocking revelation to someone who has an extremely high opinion of herself and sets herself high standards of behaviour. Miss Bates, on the other hand, is made newly aware of her inferior social status.

This is a defining moment in the story, the one which finally gets Emma to realise how smug and self-satisfied she can be, and which makes her want to become a better, kinder person, the woman Mr Knightley will want to marry.

If your story contains *big* life events like births, marriages or deaths, try to make sure they justify the space they take up in your narrative by having something dramatic happen at the same time.

Or use them to change the direction of your story.

Jane Eyre is about to get married to Mr Rochester, but the arrival of the brother of the first (and still living) Mrs Rochester puts a spoke in *that* particular wheel:

'The marriage cannot go on: I declare the existence of an impediment.'

Charlotte Brontë *Jane Eyre*

If you're a noter and a sketcher, rather than a deliberate over-writer, you'll probably be asking yourself if a scene is earning its keep all the time. You'll develop the characters and situations as you write your story, and probably give yourself and your characters lots of surprises, too.

If you're a deliberate over-writer, however, you'll need to be strict with yourself and your characters, cutting scenes which don't move the action forward, which don't reveal character, or which don't tell the reader anything he or she needs to know.

Words

If you can make all your words earn their place in your story, you'll end up with a more compelling, interesting and involving piece of work.

Verbs and **nouns** are the heavy hitters in writing, so you'll always need plenty of those. A sentence containing a verb and a noun or two will give the reader information in the simplest possible way:

Children play games.

Cats chase mice.

Pigs eat anything.

Adjectives are the literary equivalent of chocolate, gadgets and shoes – they're often irresistible, but sometimes they're bad for you. They add colour and interest to your work, but they also slow the pace of your story. This can be disastrous if you're writing a fast-paced adventure in which the hero is racing to find the lost gospel or city before the bad guys do.

Here's an example of adjectives slowing pace:

The old iron key was blood-red with rust, its blade dull and streaked, its intricate and elaborately-worked bow discoloured by the inevitable grime of a great many long centuries.

This is almost certainly overdoing a description of an old key. If you're tempted to write like this, you need to keep asking yourself – what does my reader *need* to know?

Sometimes it isn't just a question of *how many* adjectives you don't need, but *where* you don't need them.

In the example below, the pairs of adjectives draw lots of attention to themselves, and not in a good way:

It's a cold, wet day. I shiver and pull on my warm, fleecy jogging-pants and thick, hooded jumper over my damp, chilled body. I head for my warm, dry car.

Adverbs also slow the pace. You'll need to use adverbs some of the time, but think of them as the seasoning in your literary cooking, not as a main ingredient. They're useful when they're needed – for example, when you want to qualify a verb or to refine its meaning:

I don't *usually* come this way into town.
You must not drive so *carelessly*.
He *occasionally* drinks spirits.

But you will almost never need to write anything as involved as this:

I walked slowly and hesitantly down the darkening alley, breathing harshly and laboriously, hopefully trying to be quiet but fearfully fretting that I was noisily and dangerously announcing my presence.

If you can use a strong, appropriate verb in the right place at the right time, this will probably be more effective than using half a dozen adjectives or adverbs. But don't feel you need to use strong verbs like *screamed, howled* or *shrieked* all the time, especially if *asked* or *said* will do, because you'll risk making your characters seem hysterical, and your writing might look overblown.

Think about the effect you would like your story to have on your reader, and about what emotion(s) the reader might want to feel while reading it.

Thrillers and mystery stories, for example, often use lots of action verbs – people *zoom, scream, race* or *hurtle* to their destinations rather than merely *go*. These action verbs add to the excitement – and excitement is the emotion most readers of thrillers and mysteries want to feel.

But romantic heroes and heroines rarely need to *zoom* or *hurtle* anywhere.

What about *just, now, but, so, and* – these five little words tend to be over-used by all of us. They're useful because they can add nuances of meaning to your narrative, but try not to start every other paragraph with *but, just, now, and* or *so*!

A story needs to keep moving and things have to keep happening. But this doesn't mean you must keep your characters in a state of breathless activity, because *emotional* development is often as important as *physical* action. A romantic story usually shows the characters making emotional progress, learning a lot about themselves and about the nature of love, as well as doing things like becoming world famous conductors or surviving a global conflict.

You'll also need to think about your writing style. Ask yourself – is your style suited to your story? Romantic fiction is all about emotion and feeling, whereas action or adventure stories don't always need to go into much or indeed any detail about feelings and emotions. If the big question in the story is *where is the lost painting*, that's what the reader will really want to know, probably more than what the finders of the painting thought about discovering it.

As you build your stories, think about pace and style, and try to make sure they're always appropriate.

Exercise

Write a short – a few paragraphs rather than a few pages – scene which contains a lot of action. Perhaps it features running for a bus? Or maybe there's an accident? Or there could be a crime –

maybe a burglary or a mugging? Or what might happen when a lion escapes from the zoo?

Once you have written your scene, use it as a starting point for various kinds of stories. Try reworking it with different characters in different situations. Alter your sentence construction, perhaps making it more complex, perhaps simplifying it. Use more (or less) dialogue and more (or less) description. Try increasing the pace and slowing it down. Change the point of view. Try looking through the eyes of:

1 - A victim
2 - A witness
3 - A perpetrator
4 - A bus driver

Try writing your scene without using any adjectives or adverbs. What is lost and what is gained? Can you strengthen your verbs?

Consider the following three sentences:

1 - He went through the door quickly.
2 - He ran through the door.
3 - He dashed through the door.

We're not insisting any one sentence might be *better* than another. You need to decide what form of words suits your style and scene best.

Use the few paragraphs you have as tools for experimentation, and keep all your drafts to compare the results.

CHAPTER 4

Pitfalls

Here are just a few:

Falling in love with every word
Over-writing
Nice word, wrong style
Telling, not showing
Repetition
Over-explanation: a bit like repetition
Letting the literal truth get in the way
Generalisation
Clichés and other hackneyed expressions
Thinking you know the right way
Leaving out vital information
**Believing you, the well-read author, always
know best**

It must be love

Every now and then, creative writing teachers
spot a particular gleam in a student's eye. It isn't

a gleam of excitement about the subject. The student hasn't suddenly had a brilliant inspiration. It's something apparently positive but potentially harmful.

The student has fallen in love. Not with a fellow student, or with the teacher (although that is possible), but with every word they write. Every single word, from *it* to *apocalyptic*, is the student's very own baby and must not be harmed.

With any luck, this is merely an infatuation and it won't last long. If the student is in a group, the teacher's careful handling of the love-sick one is usually supported by the other students. But the lone writer at home is far more likely to have a protracted affair.

It can be energising and motivating to write without allowing your internal editor to interfere. But, at some stage, learning to edit your work is going to be imperative.

As we have already pointed out, thinking about character, dialogue, plot and narrative viewpoint is essential when you are getting to grips with the *craft* of writing. Use these four elements well and you will probably end up with an effective story.

The key word here is *effective*. In the early stages of your writing career it would be a mistake always to think in terms of *good* or *bad* writing, particularly if you are toning up your writing muscles and trying out different techniques, styles and genres. But it is very useful to ask yourself if your writing is as *effective* as you hope it might be.

As children, we learn best through play. When we are very small, play is an unstructured activity, experimental, imaginative, and we give little thought to the outcome. Gradually, however, more formal games with rules and results become the norm.

This is also true of our writing, and it's a good thing, too.

If you are writing in order to communicate, there needs to be a commonality of understanding. At various stages in our lives, most of us need to write thank you letters, business proposals and maybe coherent essays – that's if we wish to keep our friends, get decent jobs and pass exams. In all these circumstances, intellect certainly comes into play, while imagination is perhaps not quite as important.

But storytelling requires the imagination and the intellect to work *together*, not to allow one to overshadow the other. In the early stages, this relationship can take a while to settle down.

Creative writing teachers see the results of unhappy unions all the time.

What do you make of this passage below?

Over-writing…
…or contributing more to the page in terms of word count, complexity of syntax and vocabulary than might be thought or deemed strictly necessary, or indeed, in any conceivable way, desirable, is not going to advance or move forward the novice student in his or her authorial accomplishment.

There is much in this sentence that could be left out or rephrased, probably resulting in greater clarity.

As for fabulously constructed metaphors, teetering towers of adjectives and similes as smooth as the steel cladding on a skyscraper – these can be very pleasurable to read, but they draw attention to themselves. Then, the *point* of a particular passage might be lost.

Experimenting with language and finding different ways to express ideas are all part of the creative writing brief – and sometimes brief is best. Redrafting and reworking are often essential. Perhaps you have thought of ten different metaphors to describe a beautiful sunset. But a reader will understand what you mean if you use just one. So do you actually *need* more? It is advisable to keep the question of *need* in mind!

This is where asking the *effectiveness* question is a good plan. What sort of story are you writing? If it's a learned monograph, then yes, complexity might be a requirement, but your readers will no doubt be familiar with academic jargon and will probably be small in number. Remember that while a lofty style might make the author look clever, it could also affect fluency and leave the reader confused, alienated and probably not anxious to read the rest of your story.

Yet more words...

We have given you an illustration of over-writing at single sentence level. Also common, particularly at the beginning of a story, is larger scale over-writing, unkindly called information-dumping.

This is usually the result of the author informing himself or herself about a character or setting. All writers of fiction need to bear in mind that complex back-stories of minor characters, highly descriptive accounts of places or journeys, and reasons why every character is where/what/how they are, act like black holes, absorbing light and pace.

If we are told everything there is to know in Chapter 1 of a novel or on the opening page of a short story, there's going to be little room for later revelation – and gradual revelation is one of the more desirable elements of story-telling.

Nice words, wrong style or setting

Unusual, archaic or inappropriate words act like sudden braking or even emergency stops on your reader's journey through your story.

*After checking her emails, Tracy took the baby out in the **perambulator**.*

Out in the what? Which century are we in?

Whereas Nanny was required to push her charge in the perambulator but she couldn't help sighing whenever a hansom cab passed by doesn't seem so odd.

*On the mantelpiece, **a metal contraption** with a flex and shade blazed into light when switched on.*

Please! It's a lamp! But – *the room was dark as pitch. Holding his hands out he felt for the cool marble of the mantelpiece and further fumbling found a metal contraption with, yes, a flex and a shade. It blazed into light when switched on* – is fine.

*The **susurration** in the next room grew loud.*

An excellent word. It sounds like its meaning – indistinct whispering or rustling. Sometimes only one particular word will do.

Showing, not telling

Show; don't tell is a phrase the student writer hears all too frequently. It causes considerable worry and confusion. But it needn't. Stories require both telling *and* showing, but too much telling can make readers feel as if they are being given a lecture.

If you write *Tom was very tall* you are telling us something we will understand.

But now consider:

Tom banged his head every time he went through a door.
Tom pulled up the trousers of his spacesuit. As usual, a band of flesh flashed between the turn-ups and his socks.
Thank you for your enquiry about the Mars expedition, Tom read, but the Health and Safety regulations state that no astronaut should be more than six foot seven inches tall.

These three examples give us a direct understanding of how tall Tom is. Can you imagine Tom more clearly now?

Let's look again at the first example. While *Tom banged his head every time he went through a door* is more visually arresting than *Tom was very tall*, it is still a case of the author *telling* the reader. The reader has to imagine the pain of a bang on a head and also the myriad doors Tom has ever walked through. What about:

Tom ducked to get through the door of the space capsule but he didn't bend low enough. Pain exploded in a thousand stars before his eyes. Not again, he thought. When will I ever learn?

Of course, writing a short passage like the one above requires more thought and effort than merely writing *Tom was very tall*. Also, there are times when *Tom was very tall* might do very well, and anything more would fall foul of our advice about over-writing. But in the last example we now have a direct experience of Tom's height and we understand what he feels and thinks about it. We have been shown, not told.

Repetition

All teachers know they have to repeat themselves. There is an old adage that says *tell them* (your students) *what you are about to tell them, tell them, then tell them what you just told them.*

If you wish to impart information, **repetition** is a useful tool. But, like a chain saw, it requires respectful handling.

Nobody would write *John had brown hair, John's hair was brown, brown was the colour of John's hair* in a story unless they had a very good reason for doing so. But repetition can mar a story in other, more subtle ways.

The following is an exaggerated example:

John decided to go to the supermarket. He got in the car and drove to the supermarket. He parked in the car park. In the supermarket he filled up a trolley. He filled the trolley with enough food to last at least a month. He didn't like shopping much and he didn't want to have to come to the supermarket every week. He was very glad to get back home with all his shopping. John ate well that evening.

In the paragraph above, not only are words and phrases unnecessarily repeated, but also the repetition and the sentence construction result in an immature, childish style. It is a *He He He* paragraph. The same subject opens every sentence.

Sequences of paragraphs or sentences which all begin with *he, she, it, they* and *the* are common in the work of beginners and, while the vibrant content of the actual writing might make the work successful, it's worth looking to see if it's possible to add a little sparkle by doing some rearranging. One of the markers of interesting prose is a variety of sentence construction (or, a variety of sentence construction is one of the markers of interesting prose).

Sometimes, when an author wants to make a particularly strong impression, he or she might use lots of deliberate repetition. Consider this extract from *Bleak House* by Charles Dickens:

'Dead, your Majesty. Dead, my Lords and gentlemen. Dead, Right Reverends and Wrong Reverends of every order. Dead, men and women, born with Heavenly compassion in your hearts. And dying thus around us every day.'

It uses a very effective repetitive tool, alliteration: the repetition of consonants at the beginnings of words. D for *dead* certainly, but also for *dying* and *day*. R for *Right*, *(W)rong* and *Reverend*.
The idea of *Right* and *(W)rong Reverends* is deliciously wry and suggests another effective way of using repetition: it can be amusing.

Tom couldn't resist listening to it again. He turned up the volume of his iPod and shut his eyes
On the console a little red light began to wink and a tinny voice spoke through the other headphones lying on the desk.
'Hello, Tom. Houston speaking. Are you receiving me?'
The music swelled in Tom's ears. David Bowie, another starman – he knew all about space. Tom hummed along, oblivious to everything around him.
'Hello, Tom. Houston speaking. Are you receiving me?'

Tom knew it was only a matter of time, of lengthening the trousers on his space suit. One day, he'd be sitting in a tin can along with David Bowie.

'Tom! Houston speaking. Are you receiving...'

The red light went out. The track finished. Tom sighed and opened his eyes. No sign of activity on the console. But then the red light began winking rapidly. Tom swapped headphones in one quick flourish.

''ound control to Major Tom,' sang the tinny voice. Tom gasped. David Bowie was surely a god!

Every advertising copywriter knows repetition is useful because it draws attention to itself. So, if that's the effect you want, fine. But it's worth remembering that using a word or phrase twice can look like you've made a mistake or been lazy, whereas using it a third time reassures:

That night the sea raged, whipped up by the wind, black waves muscling over the sea wall and frothing across the prom. It raged past the boarded-up ice cream kiosk, the bus shelter, over the Welcome to Dawlish flower bed, until it crossed the road, lost its way and pulled back leaving nothing but a line of sand under the window of Tom's flat. Inside, nose to glass, Tom raged against the weather, the world and Sarah Jones from finance, who had turned him down yet again.

Look who's talking...

As for when you are writing dialogue and need to make it clear who is talking – does it matter if you write *said, said, said* over and over again, or should you aim for variety?

Compare and contrast the following:

Example 1:
It was no good. Tom needed help so he decided to go to the library.
'Hello?' he enquired. 'Is anybody there?'
'Yes, I am,' affirmed Jane, 'but please keep your voice down.'
'I'm looking for a book,' he whispered, 'about building a spaceship.'
'What sort of spaceship?' she quizzed.
'One that will get as far as Mars,' he explained.
'Try DIY,' she replied. 'Over there on the right.'

Example 2:
It was no good. Tom needed help so he decided to go to the library.
'Hello?' he said. 'Is anybody there?'
'Yes, I am,' said Jane, 'but please keep your voice down.'
'I'm looking for a book about building a spaceship.'

'What sort of spaceship?'
'One that will get as far as Mars,' he said.
'Try DIY. Over there on the right.'

In the first example, the pace is slowed considerably by the insertion of so many speech qualifiers. In the second example the word *said* almost disappears. It merely reminds the reader who is speaking, and that's all it needs to do.

It's also worth noting that a new paragraph indicates a new voice. So we don't need to write *said* every time someone speaks. In the above example it is self-evident.

But, if there were *several* characters standing at the library desk, and if each of them had their own ideas about where Tom should look for his book, you *would* need to make it clear who was who, and some variation on *said* might be desirable.

Over-explanation or saying the same thing or something quite like it, in another way,

perhaps over and over again.

This is repetition in disguise.
Below is an example of over-writing of the kind creative writing teachers see all the time:

It's very cold out. The wind icy <u>and freezing</u>. I'm glad I've put on my warm overcoat. I have to get to the supermarket before it shuts, otherwise there'll be no dinner.
There's a new one opening soon <u>near the big swimming pool on the corner of Church Street by the station.</u> It will be much more convenient for me to go there. I look forward to it opening. <u>I've heard it's going to be soon.</u>
I haven't yet made up my mind what to buy for supper. I fancy fish, but the kids <u>always</u> moan unless it's with chips. Bob's not keen either. He'd <u>always</u> rather have a great big steak, one of those that covers the whole plate <u>so there's no room for anything else.</u> <u>The</u> wind is whipping up, <u>getting stronger by the feel of it.</u> Maybe it will snow.

What's the matter with this passage?

The phrases underlined are either repetitious or redundant.

The location of the new supermarket is a good example of unnecessary explanation. Excellent directions, bus numbers and the times of trains, boats and planes to imaginary destinations are often included in students' work. Where these are relevant and add authenticity to a piece, they're all to the good. In this case, however, saying the supermarket is *more convenient* is enough, and providing one rather than three points of location would be sufficient. A case could be made for leaving them in only if all three locations are significant in the story.

Nothing but the truth

Oh no, not the truth again! How it gets in the way. Yes, it's a good plan to write what you know. Well, up to a point! But, if you're writing fiction, don't let the literal truth distract you or prevent you from altering the facts to suit your story.

It's not unknown for a student to be shocked when a teacher suggests doing this. The student will say *but my brother/teacher/boss would never have done that* even though the character *based* on their brother/teacher/boss desperately needs to do that very thing.

The challenge for all writers of fiction is to tell the *general* truth about human nature in all sorts of *interesting* and *unexpected* ways.

If everything that's happened in your own life really does add up to a jolly good story, perhaps you should be writing your autobiography, rather than (or as well as) fiction?

Generalisation

Tom went to the shops. The weather was awful. He met Penny, a girl he vaguely knew. She smiled at him and he asked her for a date. She said yes, and they arranged a time and place. He went home happy but then remembered he'd forgotten to do any shopping.

Could this be any more tedious? Poor Tom, no wonder he wants to go to Mars. What is so seriously lacking here is any *specific* information. Clearly, we don't need a complete résumé of Tom's activities – for example, how many and what sort of shops he went to, or detailed descriptions of the weather – but does he ask out *every* girl who smiles at him? What was it he liked about Penny? Where are they going on their date? Cape Canaveral or the Ideal Home Exhibition?

Imagine a film being made with the camera always at the same distance from the action – no aerial views, no panning back or forward, no close-ups. Yes, the story could be told, but it is the *specifics* which would have the most resonance.

'What's she like?' Tom asked Howard.
'She's great!'
'Yeah?'
'Really fantastic. Beautiful, amazing and fantastic.'
'And?'
'You'll like her, you really will.'
'That's good,' said Tom, looking doubtful. 'Does she like Dr Who?'

Here, Tom's own question about Dr Who reveals more about Tom than either of the other two characters in this extract do.

Missing something?

Most novice writers feel the need to include more detail than is necessary, but occasionally the opposite is true. While an essential element of a good detective story is the cunning withholding of information from the reader, not providing *any* information and then introducing the murderer in Chapter 29 of 30 is another crime – that of not playing fair.

Supposing Dickens *hadn't* opened *Great Expectations* with the marvellous scene in which Pip meets the convict, Magwitch? What if we, the readers, had no reason to believe or even to suspect, Miss Havisham *wasn't* Pip's benefactor? Then, hey presto, Magwitch popped up in the penultimate chapter and was revealed to be a convict Pip had helped when he was a boy *prior to the opening of the book*? Magwitch would then become a plot device, an easy solution, and all the pathos of the book would be lost.

Who was the man in the shadows? What was the knocking sound coming from the basement? Why did Harry Potter have a scar? It has to be remembered that most readers aren't psychics. Yes, it's a good idea to withhold information in the name of building tension, but at some point the reader has to know. Last page revelations can be cathartic, but you do have to get your readers there. If you have starved these readers rather than offered them an occasional snack – or, even better, one or two square meals – they may seek sustenance elsewhere.

Right or wrong?

Oh dear. A great many students worry about being wrong. They ask questions which begin *Is it all right if I...?* or *Should I...?* or *Am I allowed to...?*

A week or two later they'll be complaining, pointing out *you said I shouldn't do that!*
And they're probably right to feel aggrieved.

Sometimes, albeit rarely, a piece of writing that contains little plot, poor characterisation or terrible, clunky dialogue isn't dead in the water, but skips about on the surface making faces at us leaden-footed writers on the shore. This sort of writing is a rare being, though – and almost worthy of worship.

Do you know best?

Of course there's a right way, says the occasional student. *I know this because I've spent my life reading everything there is to know about writing, rather than actually doing much writing myself.*

If this sounds like you, beware!

Exercise

Rewrite: *Tom went to the shops. The weather was awful. He met Penny, a girl he vaguely knew. She smiled at him and he asked her for a date. She said yes, and they arranged a time and place. He went home happy but then remembered he'd forgotten to do any shopping.*

Include specific detail about the shops, Tom and Penny, the weather and where they are going. Write their dialogue. Then redraft what you have written, taking out all unnecessary repetition, adjectives and adverbs.

Then write about their date. What went right?
What went wrong? What happened in the end?

CHAPTER 5

Flash fiction and short stories

How long is short?

The first piece of prose a creative writing student produces is usually a short story rather than a novel. Short in this instance can mean anything from 500 to 5,000 words.

What do we mean by flash fiction and how does it differ from a short story?

Sometimes known as a *short short story*, flash fiction is also called *micro* or *nano fiction*. It can vary in length from five to a few hundred words. Flash fiction, while not a new form, has become increasingly popular in the last few years. The Internet has many websites devoted to its charms and competitions abound. When entering these competitions, an *exact* word count is sometimes mandatory.

Both flash and short stories are (or should be) carefully crafted and can take hours, weeks or even months to construct. They are read in minutes, usually in just one sitting. But most fans of short fiction feel these minutes are often well spent, adding something special to their day.

Apart from length, what are the differences between a novel and a short story?

Short stories don't offer the reader *long-term* involvement and excitement. They don't feature the thrill of cliffhangers at the ends of chapters, which are there to encourage the reader to turn the page and/or pick up the book up again. A short story isn't carried around for weeks while the action and all its consequences play out.

A good short story makes itself comfortable in the memory in much the same way as a good poem. As a virtual and benign guided missile, a short story can deliver a powerful emotional punch and/or be intellectually stimulating as well as satisfying.

Short stories

If you're determined to become a successful writer of short stories, we advise you to be voracious in your reading of them. While you're finding your niche and while you're exploring your own strengths and weaknesses, read every short story that comes your way. Try to work out what kind of story most appeals to you – action-packed, reflective, intellectually-challenging, emotional, philosophical, humorous, complex, simple and direct?

If you decide you wish to write for women's magazines, which is the biggest – indeed, practically the only – commercial market for short fiction in the UK, do your homework. Read the magazines to which you are going to submit your work, read their submission guidelines, and then adhere to these guidelines. If your story doesn't fit the bill, the magazine won't take it.

When students first start writing short stories, they sometimes say things like *I know this isn't very good, but I thought it might be suitable for a women's magazine.*

So – what do these students mean and what assumptions are they making? That women's magazines publish only mindless rubbish? That the editors of women's magazines are so desperate for copy they'll publish anything, however bad? That readers of women's magazines are so stupid and uncritical they will read everything the author is happy to share?

It doesn't work like that!

Who exactly reads these magazines? The advertising and features will give you some clues. What *kinds* of stories do readers enjoy? You'll need to study twenty or thirty examples from one specific title before you can hope to find out.

How long are the stories, how old are the characters, and in what sorts of life situations do they find themselves? Don't *guess* – read the magazines, and then you will *know* if writing this kind of commercial fiction is right for you.

This is a useful link for aspiring writers of women's magazine fiction – http://womagwriter.blogspot.co.uk/.

By the way – if you want to write for mostly female readers, you don't have to be female yourself. Being male need not hold you back, and don't worry, you won't have to write hearts and flowers romance if that's not your thing. Crime, mystery and even science fiction stories are published by these magazines both in the UK and in other territories world wide.

If you wish to write literary rather than commercial, mainly women's-interest short stories, you will probably find it's hard to interest the mainstream publishing industry in your work. But it's not impossible. Some independent publishers such as Salt – http://www.saltpublishing.com – have always championed the short story. The web is awash with short stories because, at last, writers themselves can place these in the public domain. Most literary writers enter their stories for competitions, which we will discuss in Chapter 7.

Short stories may contain many of the attributes of a novel – a sense of place, strong characters, dialogue, action and consequences. They are, however, unlikely to feature a large cast, several subplots or an exploration of philosophical ideas.

But Grace Paley's *Conversation with my Father* is a complex and multi-layered story which comments on the writing of a short story and is well worth reading. You can also listen to the free podcast here:
http://www.guardian.co.uk/books/audio/2010/dec/07/alismith-short-stories

Beginnings

It's very common for a novice student to ask if any piece of creative writing which comes out at longer than a few hundred words is a short story. The answer is often no because there is no actual story. A large percentage of competition entries don't get anywhere because the essential story-telling, cause-and-effect, actions-followed-by-results elements are either completely absent or are very weak. Instead, the competition judge is confronted with an excellent descriptive piece or a character sketch. Reading a story of this sort is a bit like getting into the passenger seat of a car only to have the driver draw your attention to the interior features, but then get out and walk away.

Sometimes, the writer realises that there is no plot and shoe-horns the whole story into the final paragraph:

Tom woke early on the morning of the rocket launch. The sun speared through the curtains, straight into his eyes... (another 250 words about getting out of bed and ablutions)
Bacon, sausage and a fried egg for breakfast. Yummy, thought Tom. This might not be the wisest breakfast to have before experiencing 3g in the shuttle but it may be my last, so I'll risk it...(250 more words on the virtues of a full English breakfast)
Tom took a taxi to the launch pad. The driver told him a story about another astronaut he'd taken to the space centre. What happened was...(indeterminate number of words)

Eventually, in the final paragraph, we might find:

When Tom, the only survivor, walked away from the spaceship crash, he was assumed to be a god by the population on planet Prehensile. He married the queen and she bore him several children who grew to adulthood in the equivalent of six Earth months. All the girls had useful prehensile tails but the male children had only the stunted bottoms of Earthlings. Before long a bitter gender war raged until one night Tom's wife slid her tail all the way round his neck and pulled tighter and tighter...

The End

How about beginning that story when the spaceship crashes? Has anyone survived? Only one: lucky Tom, who was thrown clear on impact still strapped to his seat. Maybe we could find out about Tom's breakfast habits as we go along? Or not, with any luck.

Let's get going

It's always difficult to decide where to begin a story. We have seen that a long preamble can at best be distracting. At worst, your reader won't stay the course.

Asking a direct question or seeding a question is a good way to involve your reader:

Am I tough enough for this mission? thought Tom, as he gazed at the sky/full English breakfast.

The postman handed Tom a large parcel. He wasn't expecting anything but there was no mistaking his name and address written in bold italics on the label. From the outside it looked as if someone had sent him a space helmet.

Letters, parcels, boxes and bags are always intriguing. Already, we'll be wondering whether Tom's parcel *does* contain a space helmet.

Anything readers can't see draws them in: *Tom looked over the wall and was astonished by what he saw…*

Or, even better, in direct speech: *'Good Heavens!' the postman said to Tom. 'Take a look at that.'*

Both of these examples seed the question: what are they looking at?

Passive statements make for rather weak openers:

It was raining/Tuesday/my school reunion.
There was a sale on in the shoe shop.
The bus was late.

But if a passive statement says something *unusual* it can work very well.

Raymond Carver opens his short story *Why Don't You Dance?* with this:
In the kitchen, he poured another drink and looked at the bedroom suite in his front yard.

Katherine Mansfield's short story *The Daughters of the Late Colonel* opens with:

The week after was one of the busiest weeks of their lives.

Both of these examples are simple sentences that beg questions. In the first, why is there a bedroom suite in the yard? We note *he* is having *another* drink. In the second, it is the presence of the word 'after' that acts as a waving flag. After what?

Be wary of generalisations that leave the reader hunting for context. For example:

He walked down the road. The rain gradually got worse and by the time he reached the traffic lights it was sheeting down. Ankle-deep puddles soon formed in the gutters and cars sent up waves of water. He put his newspaper over his head but it got soggy almost at once and was a poor substitute for an umbrella.

So far, the most we can glean from this beginning is that the setting is urban and it's a wet day. Someone walking down a road isn't a very attention-grabbing opener. If the next sentence were to be in some way remarkable this might not matter. But, sadly, it isn't at all remarkable.

We don't know the protagonist's name or whether he is twenty or eighty. Why he is walking down the road? Is he in London, Glasgow or Cape Town? As yet, nothing has happened, and if something intriguing doesn't happen very soon there's a strong possibility we might give up on this story.

A little specific information might help. What difference would it make if he sheltered under *The Times*? Or *The New York Times*? Or *The Financial Times*? Perhaps nothing, perhaps everything. What difference would it make to readers if they knew his name was Cedric or Hassan? Or Prince Charming?

But don't worry too much and don't let the hunt for a good first line prevent you from getting started. Writing a story is a slippery business at the best of times and so, if you have an idea about where your story goes rather than how it begins, we suggest you get going and sort out the first line, paragraph or first thousand words later.

Moving on

It's worth remembering that taking one step back means you'll need to take two steps to move forward again.

Tom ambled towards the nursery. He remembered running down that same corridor for the first time five children ago. It had been a dark and stormy night and the roof on the banana store had blown away. The second time, it was foggy...

We're already afraid Tom might need to remember what the weather was like on each of the five previous occasions he's walked to the nursery, and that's before we get back to the present...

If some back-story is *necessary*, that's fine. Perhaps the weather has religious significance on this planet, or babies' names are weather-related.

In Chapter 2 we considered what makes a story. In addition to thinking about the points made there, it's worth asking your story itself a few questions, either as you go along or when you have finished the first draft.

For example:

1 - How old and from what social class or educational background is your ideal reader?
2 - What sort of story is it – action-packed, reflective, philosophical, simple, complex?
3 - When and where is it set?
4 - Whose story is it?

5 - If you were to sum up your main character in two or three words, what would they be?

6 - Do you need every character?

7 - Is it wise to name your characters Ted, Ed and Ned or Joan, Jane and Jan? And consider Alex, Sam and Chris carefully, too. Male or female?

8 - What problems do the characters face?

9 - What attributes do they reveal in trying to overcome them? Perhaps bravery impatience and/or cruelty?

10 - What are you going to hold back from revealing, so the reader keeps reading in order to find out what this could be?

11 - What does the main character learn/realise/overcome by the end?

12 - What has changed by the end of your story?

Some of those twelve questions might be inappropriate. But, if you feel they could be pertinent and you have trouble answering them, try to put yourself in the heads of your readers. Are you communicating what you want to communicate? Do you actually want your readers to *struggle* to understand your story? Do you think they will bother?

This isn't to say your writing must be so transparent as to be bland. But clarity and accessibility are desirable in any kind of fiction. So don't make your writing obscure or convoluted because you think doing this will make you sound intelligent, and don't sacrifice content to style.

Stories which are all style and no substance can be very disappointing. Tom the astronaut's breakfast could be a banquet, eloquently described to the point of tasting which side of the bush the sage leaf in the sausages came from, but we'll still want to know what happened *after* breakfast.

So – what *did* happen? Perhaps we found out more about the warring Prehensiles? Maybe Tom's indigestion was so bad he never made it to the launch pad? How disappointing that would have been – for readers and for him.

Let us assume Tom didn't feel too bad. What became of him next? Later, what problem(s) did he have to overcome – was it one big problem or a several small ones?

Who are your readers and what might they want?

As for your target readership – if you happened to be a reader who loved science fiction, in particular stories about space travel, by now you'd probably be very fed up with Tom.

But most other readers probably wouldn't be very happy, either. If Tom's indigestion turned out to be a rare disease, difficult to diagnose, and Tom was suddenly at the centre of a thrilling life-and-death medical drama, fans of medical dramas might never have got to read your story because at the beginning they would have been so seriously misled. If Tom and Penny ended up blasting off into a happy sunset and setting up home in a country cottage, rather than taking a spaceship to Mars, romance readers wouldn't know about it because they wouldn't have got that far into the story.

Do some market analysis and ask yourself it you would you send your own story to *Stethoscope Monthly* magazine or *Rocket Romantics*? Ask yourself what *sort* of story you want to write and then try to work out what kind of readership might enjoy it.

Endings

What happens in the end?

Here are five possibilities.

1 - They find the treasure/murderer/missing child/way home/secret of the universe.
2 - They get married/realise they love/can't stand each other.
3 - They realise they've been wrong/deluded/misled/wicked/right all the time.
4 - They repent/celebrate/go and live in a cave.
5 - They die and go to Heaven/Purgatory/the Grey Havens.

Of course, *they* could also be *she, he* or the alien equivalent.

Doesn't a short story have to have a twist in the tale?
Not always. But students often write stories which have a twist welded on to the last paragraph. Surprise! He was really a dentist, terrorist, transvestite, prehensile, after all. Or she did it because she was jealous, mad, drunk or the bastard child of royalty.

The ending of a story needs to reveal what happened as a *result* of the *action* which has gone before. So a sudden revelation could be seen as cheating. Yes, delivering this kind of ending might be very tempting if you have plotted your

way into a dead end and/or come up against a brick wall. But a *satisfying* twist has its seed planted early on and its roots embedded during the story. Talking of walls, *The Yellow Wallpaper* by Charlotte Perkins Gilman contains a fine example of a great twist in the tale. It's downloadable for free here:
http://www.gutenberg.org/ebooks/1952

Flash Fiction

This is a short, short story with all (or most of) the characteristics of its longer sibling. Storytelling is still to the fore, but brevity requires much to be suggested or implied.

Small on the page; big in the mind – this is a good maxim.

One example, sometimes attributed to Ernest Hemingway, is:

For sale: baby shoes, never worn.

A sad tale comes immediately to mind. We may not know the details of what happened, but something has clearly gone very wrong. Was there a death? A sudden illness? A kidnap? Time has passed in these six words. There was hope for those little shoes but it was dashed. Now they are for sale. Not given or thrown away. Someone must need the money.

How different this story would be if the word *baby* had been left out: *For sale: shoes, never worn.* Also, consider how different it would be if it were to read: *For sale: baby shoes, worn.*

In a very short piece of flash fiction every single word matters:

They both fell: she – over his suitcase, he – head over his heels.

Out of the sea, down from the trees, into Marks and Spencer!

Fortunately for us, most flash stories are longer than a dozen words and we can luxuriate in a couple of hundred or more.

What about creating a world or alternative reality for the reader, how does something as short as a short story or a piece of flash fiction manage to do that?

A determined author can take the reader there in a very few well-chosen words and phrases. See how successfully Exeter Novel Prize winner **Su Bristow** creates a sense of place in her short short story *Train*:

Train

We waited, huddled in the long grass. It'll turn your sixpences into shillings, they'd said. There was no sound yet, other than our own too-loud breathing, and the everlasting larks that you could hear but never see.

Sally clutched at my arm. The rails were singing! She dug her nails into me, and I didn't shake her off. The sound grew, like distant starlings. A rising rumble, a vibration in your bones, and then the great black whoosh of it tearing a hole through the world. And it was gone, leaving nothing but a stain on the air.

Shakily, we climbed down to the tracks. They'd told us wrong. Hers was bent, misshapen, useless. Mine, strangely, was not changed at all. The larks exulted, on and on.

Let's look at how this story of one hundred and twenty-seven words, not counting the title, has been constructed.

In the beginning, the scene is set by the title and the first sentence. An immediate intrigue is set up in the second. Tension is created with *too-loud breathing* and *Sally clutched at my arm* and *dug her nails into me, and I didn't shake her off.*

In the middle, something happens – there's exciting action which is, in the end, life-changing. It's suggested how life (the train) will be for the two children (the two sixpences) and that the universe (the larks) is indifferent to our fate. This story is a lesson in not believing every thing we are told.

So here we have the classic three section story structure: **set-up**, **action** and **consequence**, with a dash of **enigma** to make us think.

Short stories don't have to be obvious and explicit. They can also imply, and trust the reader to pick up on the implication. The shorter the story, the more implication might be needed. It will require deft handling. If your readers have to do too much work, you might lose them. Imagine you're going on a treasure hunt. How would you feel if vital clues were missing, which meant the treasure was impossible to find?

In the following story, the protagonist appears to take against her neighbours because they have their television on too loud and they shop at a supermarket *she* does not frequent. But that isn't the *real* reason she doesn't want to invite them back for tea.

Every morning Linda drank tea from a cup and saucer, the last of her grandmother's favourite set. How maddening then, to break the cup. She haunted charity shops.

When new people moved in next door they invited her in and lo, their dresser bore a single cup bearing the same rosy pattern.

'Oh!' said Linda, 'I have the saucer.'

'Do you?' replied her neighbour. 'That's wonderful! I've been searching for one for ages.'

Linda did not reply.

At home, she gave the saucer on her own dresser a hard stare. A return invitation would have to be issued soon.

But weeks went by. Their television clapped and chatted through the wall and shopping deliveries came from a supermarket Linda never frequented. What a relief she hadn't invited them back. Clearly they weren't her cup of tea at all.

Cathie Hartigan *Weak or Strong*

Writing flash is both illuminating and entertaining, but it should be remembered that flash fiction isn't merely a synopsis of a longer story. It needs to be well-crafted and emotionally compelling, too.

Do we need to know?

As creative writing teachers and judges of competitions, we have been fortunate enough to read thousands of short stories. We have enjoyed most of them and learned a great deal about what works and what doesn't, fiction-wise.

But something which increasingly saddens, worries and can also bore us is the increase in disturbing or sensationalist content that has little bearing on the actual story.

Does a story have to be bleak and miserable in order to be meaningful? Too often we have been confronted with casual murder, child abuse, sexual violence and cruelty of the most imaginative kind for no good reason. We repeat – *no good reason*.

We are not squeamish wimps who faint at the sight of a swear word or a bloodstained corpse. We are not suggesting that the above elements should never be present in a story. But *a description of a murder or an abusive sex scene isn't a story in itself,* although the prelude and/or repercussions might well be.

It's worth noting that gratuitous sex and violence can seriously mar your story rather than enhance its chances of success. So ask yourself if these elements are *relevant* before you include them in a story. What actually *needs* to be there?

Exercise

Try writing a story then reducing it by at least half. If you have a story already written, so much the better because you will have written it without this exercise in mind.

Once you have halved the word count, halve it again. What do you want to retain and why? What can be stripped out without losing a) the meaning and b) the story's charm?

Begin by asking yourself if whole scenes are necessary. Cut big sections first, then sentences, then single words.

CHAPTER 6

Novels

Novellas
What is a novel?
Characters
Openings and prologues
On with the story
Resolutions

If you've decided that creatively-speaking you're a long distance runner as opposed to a sprinter, you're probably going to want to write **novels** rather than **flash fiction**, **short stories** or even **novellas**.

What is a novella?

It's a story which doesn't always have the depth and complexity of a full-length novel, but is much longer and more involved than a short story. It allows for sub-plotting and there's more scope for character development than is usual in a short story. It's much closer in form to the novel than to the short story. The notes on novels which you will find in this chapter also apply to the novella.

A novella is typically between about 15,000 and 50,000 words long, but these limits are flexible and some novellas are very short – hardly longer than a traditional short story.

Many novellas are available as ebooks from the usual sources such as Amazon and Smashwords. Most women's magazine serials are round about novella-length and some are also published as large print or ebooks.

The novella has a long and respectable literary history. Here are some famous examples – Charles Dickens *A Christmas Carol*, Philip Roth *Goodbye, Columbus*, and Joseph Conrad *The Secret Sharer*. It's been argued that Julian Barnes's Booker Prize winning novel *The Sense of an Ending* is really a novella, coming in at about 150 printed pages – see http://www.guardian.co.uk/books/booksblog/2011/oct/20/booker-prize.

Of course, some authors write and are published across the whole spectrum of fiction. They're equally adept at flash fiction, short stories, novellas and novels. But most of us find we have a natural affinity with just one or two kinds of story-telling. So we work hard at getting better and better in our chosen fields.

What is a novel?

It's a story which is between about 50,000 and 150,000 words long. These numbers aren't set in stone, but nowadays a commercial print publisher will probably be reluctant to consider anything shorter than about 50,000 or longer than about 150,000 words unless there is something very special and commercially attractive about the story or the author or both.

These restrictions are partly down to the economics of print (as opposed to digital) publishing. A very short book can look like poor value for money and most people like to get good value for their hard-earned cash. A print publisher's production costs aren't going to be significantly lower than usual even if a novel *does* come in at under 50,000 words. As for novels over 150,000 words long – they're bulky, they're heavy, they take up *lots* of warehouse and bookshop shelf space, they don't fit easily into pockets or handbags, and the paperback editions tend to fall apart.

So – if you want to see your novel commercially published as a print book, as opposed to an ebook, we advise you to go for a length of between 50,000 and 150,000 words – no less and certainly no more. About 80,000 – 120,000 words are going to be fine for most commercial print publishers. But, if you're aiming to submit to specific publishers, always check their requirements first.

What if you intend to write a *series* of novels, as Stephenie Meyer must have done when she planned the Twilight series, and J K Rowling certainly did when she planned the Harry Potter stories?

This is fine, because most readers love series. But you'll have to make sure each individual volume of your story is **complete in itself**.

What do we mean by that?

Let's look at an example or two. *Twilight* is the opening story in a series and it's complete in itself because it resolves one of the important issues. The ending of *Twilight* shows the reader that Bella and Edward are now committed to each other, whatever the risks and difficulties that lie ahead. At this point in the whole story, Bella could have walked away from Edward. But she doesn't – she makes the choice to stay with him and be part of his life.

Similarly, in the Harry Potter novels, Harry manages to hold off or to defeat Voldemort *for the time being* at the end of every volume. But of course Voldemort bounces back time after time, and isn't overcome for good until the end of the final book in the series.

So, if you too are writing a series of novels, your own first volume will need to show your characters coming to some kind of conclusion, settling some important issue, and getting ready to meet the next challenge. Series stories are somewhat like battles in a war – at the end of each volume, the reader will need to know who won that particular battle, but will be prepared to wait until the end of the series to find out who won the war.

A marathon task

A novel is a big undertaking. As a novelist, you're setting out on a long and sometimes difficult journey, so you'll need to give yourself, your characters and your readers plenty of good reasons to make this journey.

We're talking about an investment in time of several days or weeks of your reader's life, and maybe several years of your own.

How do you set about making this investment worthwhile?

By writing about interesting characters with whom the reader can identify or even fall in love, and by putting these characters in challenging, problematic, difficult, dangerous, life-threatening and/or intriguing situations.

Your reader's initial reaction to hearing about your characters and their life-situations should be: *all's not right in your world, is it? What are you going to do about it, then? How are you going to cope?*

Characters

We suggest you get going on your novel by making friends with a character or characters with whom you will want to spend lots of your time. This person or these people will have to carry your story and make the reader want to know what happens to them.

So choose a central character you like, and about whom you want to write, as Jane Austen did when she began writing *Emma*, a novel starring a heroine the author said she thought *no one but myself will much like*. If *you* love or at least like your hero and/or heroine, the chances are you will be able to persuade your readers to love or at least like these people, too – as we're sure Jane Austen knew perfectly well!

How do you encourage readers to love your characters?

If you give a character a narrative viewpoint, you'll have a much better chance of getting the reader to identify with this person. In fiction and in life, it's quite hard to dislike someone who tells us their deepest, darkest secrets. We're flattered to be trusted and to be in the know. A character who seems confident or even arrogant as far as other people in the story are concerned, but who reveals a softer, gentler, more sympathetic and more appealing side to the reader, is likely to become the reader's friend as well as your own.

So maybe spend a bit of time with your central character or characters before you write a single word of your story, getting to know these people well, making a few notes about them, and perhaps, if you're handy with a pencil, even sketching them? Then you can decide:

What they look like – are they handsome, deformed, beautiful, interesting, plain, pretty, ugly, mutilated, scarred, fat, thin, tall, short?
What they feel about their fellow men and women – do they love them, hate them, like them, or are they indifferent to them?
What religious, moral, ethical and political views they hold – if they have any, and what they might be?
What happened to them before your story starts?
What they feel about their families – are they close to their families, estranged from their families, do they even *have* families?
Where they came from – what are their ethnic and social origins?
Where and who they are now – where do they live, how do they live, what is their social class?

You'll think of many more things you would like to know, so jot them down as they come into your head – colours of eyes, colours of hair, special likes and dislikes, hopes, fears, addictions, phobias, strengths, weaknesses, names of first pets, if these people have brothers or sisters, step-mothers or step-fathers – anything that seems relevant to you.

You could also sketch out a few scenes in which they appear, and you could get them talking to you by composing a few monologues and/or by writing some dialogue between them and your other characters. Speak some of your dialogue out loud and try to *hear* how your characters speak. Do they have regional accents, are their voices soft, deep, low, harsh, loud? Do they shout, do they whisper, do they order other people around or do they try to persuade? Give them opinions of their own, which may or may not be your opinions, too.

You probably won't use all this material in your actual story. But, if you get to know your characters well, they will become real for you, and when you are writing about them you will sometimes feel as if you are taking some kind of cosmic dictation as they talk to you.

If you *don't* get to know your characters well, you could end up creating stereotypes – for example, grumpy old men, damsels in distress, wicked stepmothers, lecherous uncles, and so on.

Appealing characters are individuals, whether they are heroes or villains, mentors or facilitators, major protagonists or have minor parts to play in your story.

Looking at life

Don't worry if you find yourself taking various attributes of people you know and giving these attributes to characters of your own. Sometimes, it helps to imagine how a real person would react to a given situation, or even to remember what a real person actually said and did when he or she was bereaved, became a parent or lost a job.

But it would probably be unwise to put a whole real person into a novel. There's no knowing how this real person might react. It's likely that many of your non-writing friends, family members and acquaintances will see themselves in your stories even though they never entered your head throughout the whole writing process.

People who have limited imaginative lives themselves often seem to find it hard to believe that novelists *make things up*!

Openings...

You'll need to start your story by making lots of **promises**, which you'll then need to keep. You'll also need to ask or suggest lots of questions, such as *what's going on here, what's the problem, who is trying to hurt my hero, who is my heroine going to marry*?

Some novelists love writing **prologues**, and these can be very effective appetisers preceding the main course of your story. But you may not know if you need a prologue until *after* you have finished your novel, especially if you aren't a detailed planner.

A prologue will be useful if you feel you need to:

1 - Offer the reader some essential backstory?
2 - Drop hints about what is to come?
3 - Set the style and/or pace and/or tone of your novel, which may not be possible in Chapter 1 if this first chapter begins when all is well in a central character's life, but everything is soon going to change for the worse?
4 - Let the reader see some of the action from the point of view of somebody who is not a main viewpoint character but whose opinions are going to matter?

If you don't need to do any of these four things, you probably won't need a prologue. You'll be able to get going in the here-and-now by writing Chapter 1 and presenting your central character with something which will get your reader hooked – a challenge, a choice, an encounter with someone who is going to love him, hate him, marry him or try to kill him, or some other life-changing event which you find intriguing, and hope your reader will find intriguing, too.

As with any kind of story, you will need to suggest to your reader there's something he or she needs to find out. This is why we read any kind of fiction – to find things out. A good story both educates and entertains us. It makes information easy to absorb and thus to retain. Many of us know all we'll ever know about horses from reading *Black Beauty*, all we'll ever know about Victorian London from reading *Oliver Twist*, all we'll ever know about BDSM from reading *Fifty Shades of Grey*.

...and continuations...

When you begin your novel, you probably won't have time to do a lot of scene-setting, and you probably shouldn't even consider it. This is because you will need to get your story moving, and scene-setting is essentially static.

As citizens of the 21st century, we're accustomed to instant gratification in many aspects of our lives, including the arts. Contemporary theatre and cinema productions have taught us to become restless and impatient if a story doesn't get going straight away. We're often annoyed if we have to wait for anything to be made clear.

So, we 21st century novelists have to use plenty of narrative cunning and to entice readers into our stories by filling our shop windows – our opening pages – with exciting and wonderful things such as **crisis**, **conflict**, **challenge** and **change.**

If you feel you absolutely must set the scene and show the reader where and when the action is taking place, try to do this in *dialogue* or *monologue* while your characters are doing something important – meeting, arguing, kissing, killing, dying – or as they're asking themselves and the reader some important questions.

American novelist Eowyn Ivey manages this brilliantly in the opening of her debut novel *The Snow Child,* which begins as her heroine contemplates suicide in the Alaskan wilderness where the novel is set.

If you're writing **romantic fiction**, try to arrange for your hero and heroine to meet or at least hear of each other in the first few pages. If you're writing **crime**, **thriller** or **mystery** fiction, try to kill someone or to make something perplexing take place as soon you possibly can, because – as we've seen – these days most readers expect to get some kind of instant gratification from a story, and they become impatient if they *don't* get it.

They want to be hooked straight away, and days of the average reader being willing to slog through the first fifty pages of a novel before anything significant happens are lost in the mists of time – which is a **cliché**, by the way, and you should try to avoid clichés.

When you're writing something as long as a novel, it's easy for several dozen or even hundreds of clichés to worm their way into your prose. We can all get away with a few. But, when they *do* turn up, it's good if you can manage to subvert them or make them sound a bit more intriguing than usual.

As **cold** as what – not ice, not snow, not charity, but what about as cold as an Eskimo's vodka martini or a penguin's toes?

If you *do* take your time to get started, and if your writing *is* full of clichés, a literary agent or publisher's reader probably won't get as far as page five, let alone fifty, because these professional readers expect to be hooked, entertained and intrigued from page one.

...and pacing yourself and your story...

As you write your novel, actual physical fatigue is unlikely to kill you. But you, your characters and your readers will probably enjoy the journey more if you take frequent breaks.

Some novelists give themselves time off between chapters to write other kinds of fiction, or to update their blogs, or to catch up on Twitter and Facebook, or generally refresh themselves by doing something like walking the dog or mowing the lawn before going back to the novel-in-progress.

Some deliberately break off at an interesting, tantalising or dramatic high point, even if that point is half way through a paragraph or sentence, because they know if they do it this way they'll be keen to get back to the story.

They're also aware it can be dangerous to stop when they're flagging or they don't know what to write next. If they take a break at a critical point, the chances are they'll *never* know. It's hard to press on when the going gets tough, but professional novelists force themselves to keep moving, and promise themselves a reward when they've struggled through a difficult or challenging part of a story.

Just keep going – that's always going to be good advice to a novelist. Nobody can read a novel you haven't written. Like a lot of good advice, however, it can be difficult to take, especially when you're tired and disenchanted. Most novelists tend to be very good at finding other things to do, and on days when their writing isn't going well almost anything else can seem irresistibly attractive. But the prospect of a reward or two can give them the impetus to carry on.

...and getting it written...

As you write, don't worry too much about getting it right at first draft stage. These days, most of us compose at the computer keyboard.

This means we can move text around, expand, delete and revise at will, and we can also keep older versions of our work in case we decide we were right the first time.

It is worth setting up a dedicated online account (Google's Gmail is ideal) which will keep your mail forever. If you then send each day's output to yourself as an email attachment, it will stay on this provider's server and it will all be in date order, too – an electronic record of the development of your novel.

...and rewarding readers...

Readers need rewards in the shape of cliffhangers and questions which will keep them interested as they travel through your story. But you don't need to make your readers feel breathless and in need of a lie down. Once your readers are hooked, your action shouldn't need to zoom along at breakneck speed. You can vary the pace, and all-action scenes can be interspersed with comparatively quiet stretches where your characters are taking stock, having a break from their many trials and tribulations, or just enjoying a bit of peace and quiet before the next storm.

Readers of romantic fiction are often relieved to see the hero and heroine having some fun together before the next obstacle to everlasting happiness trips them up. Later on, making choices and meeting challenges give both author and reader a reason to continue the journey in the hope that something wonderful or fascinating will always be on the horizon.

In *Pride and Prejudice*, for example, it seems likely Mr Darcy and Elizabeth will find their own happy-ever-after when they meet at Pemberley and realise they could be ideally suited after all.

But then Lydia elopes with the wicked Mr Wickham, and it looks as if Elizabeth won't be marrying Mr Darcy now. The reader's and Elizabeth's hopes are dashed, but now they both have an incentive to continue the journey to find out what happens in the end.

...and finding resolutions

At the end of your story you will need to leave your characters in the places they want and/or deserve to be. You probably ought to know roughly where they're going, but ideally you should be flexible enough to let them give you and the reader a few surprises, too.

Storytellers have long since realised *action* arises out of *character* and *situation*. So, you should refer to your notes on your characters frequently and, as these characters develop, grow, mature and change, the action should develop, too.

Exercise

Think of a problematic situation, big or small, which might take some time and ingenuity to resolve.

Perhaps a man has lost his money, his home, his wife, his children or his dog?

Perhaps a woman has lost her job, her boyfriend, her parents, her handbag or her cat?

What will he or she do now?

You'll need to start developing a story line which takes your characters' personalities into account. How well (or badly) equipped are they when it comes to solving their problems? What obstacles are they going to face? What is going to go right for them and what is going to go wrong?

How are they going to move on?

They mustn't drag their heels but they don't need to rush. They have about 80,000 words in which to turn their lives around.

CHAPTER 7

Getting out there

Why are you writing?
Competitions
Promoting yourself
The Internet
Self-publishing

Why are you writing?

Unless you are already a celebrity, nobody is going to knock on your door and ask for your novel, story or piece of flash fiction.

Perhaps that doesn't matter because you are writing purely for your own pleasure and don't want anyone else to read your work?

But, if that's the case, why you are you reading this book?

Something inside you is interested in the writing process. Maybe you have found it hasn't gone smoothly or there's something you're not sure about? You care enough to want to improve. When this happens, it isn't long before the vast majority of people who write seek a reader. Or even lots of readers.

Competitions

One of the best ways to acquire a respectable writing CV is to win or be placed in competitions. If you google **writing competitions** you may be amazed at the number which exist. Be warned, though – it's not a good plan to enter dozens of them, and/or the ones with the most prize money, without first doing a little research.

There are several generous individuals who keep a rolling directory of competitions, often with useful bits of information attached. Some helpful links include http://www.jbwb.co.uk/writingcomps.htm and http://www.writersreign.co.uk/Short-Story-Competitions.html.

The Bridport Prize offers tempting prize money. It also offers immediate and huge kudos if you are placed. However, a little look at the previous winners reveals the calibre of the entrants. Nearly all are published already and have won other prestigious prizes. Another stark fact worth thinking about is that in 2011, according to their website, they had 11,440 online entries!

Our advice before entering any competition is: read the stories that have won in the past. Often they are on the competition website. Or you may have to buy an anthology. You aren't looking to copy the previous winners, but you may get a sense of the writing styles and subjects that tend to be successful.

But judges change and, unlike in the case of women's magazine fiction, there probably won't be any guidelines. Do check, though, just to make sure.

Our experience as competition judges is that considerable numbers of stories aren't stories at all. They might be well-written and about interesting subjects, but there is no or very little development.

The ending of a story needs to be significant even if it doesn't deliver the classic gasp/twist. Put yourself in the judges' shoes and ask yourself: is the ending of your story satisfying and/or relevant? Or does the story just stop?

What's our best advice?

It's *read the rules several times and adhere to them, down to the smallest detail.*

We know from experience that in any competition there will always be a considerable number of entries which immediately disqualify themselves because the entrants haven't obeyed the rules.

If a **theme** is mentioned, don't send an entirely unrelated story 'just in case'. Check your **presentation**. A story that is **single-spaced** when the requirement is for **double-spacing** will not be read. What a shame, to do all that work for nothing. Your **entry fee** will still be cashed, so in effect you will have **paid** somebody to open an envelope, glance at your story then **put it in the bin, even if that story is brilliant.**

If you use a very small font, your entry might not be read. 12 point Times New Roman, Arial or Bookman are ideal.

Don't make it hard for the judges to like your story.

A winning story grabs the reader's attention with the very first sentence, and retains its grip until the last

This isn't to say your story needs to shout loudly all the way through. Sometimes a small thing, a lost message or an overheard comment, is enough to hook and hold your reader.

Easy, no?

Well, it *would* be easy if we all liked the same things and our moods remained the same from day to day. But judges are human too, and a winner one day might not be a winner the next. In a competition with hundreds or perhaps thousands of entries, all the stories on the shortlist and maybe even the longlist might make worthy winners. So put *all* your own successful listings on your CV.

Promoting yourself

You might have a big family, lots of colleagues and a wide circle of friends, but if you sit down and add up the actual numbers, what's the total? Of those tens or dozens or even hundreds of people, how many do you think would open their purses or wallets and buy your book?

Celebrities have agents and publishers ringing their doorbells because many thousands, perhaps even millions, of people have heard of them – and that means big potential sales.

The **local newspaper** is the usual conduit for news and, if you have writing success in the shape of a published book or a competition win, that's news! What about sending out a press release? There is some good advice from Cake Publicity here: www.cakepublicity.co.uk/guides.php.

Your local radio station(s), both BBC and commercial, can reach even bigger numbers. They are usually keen to interview published writers, so it is well worth ringing them. If you aren't commercially published but your book/poetry/article is of local interest, still ring them. Remember that local interest could mean all sorts of things, even if your book is set on Mars. After all, *you* are local. Write down what you are going to say before you ring so that you sound attractive and appealing. Practise with a friend. This isn't being overly obsessive. It's merely being sensible.

Serendipity plays a part, but you can put yourself in its way. Self-published author Pamela Vass attended a workshop with the crime writer Simon Hall and gave him a copy of her book *Seeds of Doubt*. He liked it, recognised a strong story of local interest and, in his capacity as the crime correspondent for BBC Radio Devon, recommended her as a guest on a popular show. Consequently, she was asked to serialise her book for the station. That's a result.

Do you have any **business cards**? If you have a book to promote, what about getting bookmarks or postcards printed, featuring the cover art? Don't assume a publisher will do these things for you. Having something nice-looking to give the people you meet is more professional than handing out names or numbers on scraps of paper. If you believe in what you do, gradually the embarrassment of self-promotion will diminish.

What is going on in your area that might somehow **relate to you and your work**? Don't worry if the link is rather tenuous. Ask yourself how your presence could be of help to some other individual, group or organisation. With the answer to that in your opening gambit, ask if you can give a talk, answer questions, sign your book or give a reading.

The Internet

These days, everyone is short of funds. Publishers have had to cut their marketing budgets and they now expect authors to be energetic in promoting their own work, doing much more than a launch and a few signings.

This can be terrifying for authors who spend an enormous amount of time on their own. Most writers are very comfortable or even happy to be alone. But those who regard the sociability of the Internet with suspicion, fearing an invasion of the world every time they fire up their computers, don't realise it is vital for the promotion of their work and that, for the shy and introverted, the Internet can be their best friend.

It is not unreasonable to expect a literary agent to google the author of a submission which looks interesting. Perhaps the agent has two authors from which to choose. The author with the more attractive online presence is more likely to be of interest.

Let's imagine the first author has a **Facebook** page that is blocked to the general public, and/or a mention or two about their job which is in a field not relevant to their writing.

But the second submission comes from someone who has a **website** devoted to his or her favourite books and/or personal writing experience. The site features an up-to-date **blog** that connects to a **Facebook** page sporting five hundred friends. This same author has **Twitter** and **LinkedIn** accounts and is maybe a member of a few relevant writing or literary online groups, too.

Apart from wondering how this person finds the time to write a book at all, the agent will realise that here is someone who's serious about what they do and is willing to work at getting themselves known. From the agent's point of view, that means good potential sales.

The reality today is that nobody gets commercially published unless their work seems likely to make a profit for the publisher. Once the bestsellers might have subsidised less profitable books, but now times are hard for loss leaders, too.

Twitter

There are some people who apparently spend all their waking hours writing messages of one hundred and forty characters. You might not be one of them, but rest assured it's very easy to set up your own Twitter account. Go to www.twitter.com and follow the instructions.

If you click on a button asking to be notified when a specific person tweets anything, the chances are this person will notice and will follow you. The number of followers you acquire will depend on how much time you spend trying to attract these followers – unless of course you're already famous, in which case people will follow you without being asked.

Facebook

Facebook is a social networking site which encourages people and groups to befriend each other. Go to www.facebook.com and get started by designing your own page. You can put up photographs, too. There's plenty of information available which will help you to do this, either on Facebook's own pages or elsewhere online.

There's virtually no limit to the length of a Facebook post, so Facebook is especially popular with writers, probably because writers tend to be people who always have a lot to say and who like to keep in touch.

If you find any people you know are already on Facebook, invite them to become your Facebook friends. As your list of friends grows, your posts will become available to more and more people and you will become more widely known.

Learn how to put up links to other websites. Reply to people if they mention you. Comment on what they said. Retweet/share messages to/with all your followers/friends. But don't be irritating and/or continually try to sell something. Make it clear you're a human being, not a robot churning out spam.

LinkedIn

LinkedIn is primarily a professional networking site. The user's profile displays their curriculum vitae and members can endorse one another's skills. http://www.linkedin.com

Blogging and websites

If you're new to writing fiction and you're not yet part of a writing community, either face to face or online, you should consider joining one soon. This is because it will be useful and encouraging to meet other creative writers who also talk to imaginary people living inside their heads, and who don't think this behaviour is particularly strange – which ordinary members of the public and non-writing family members and friends often do!

You'll find a popular UK chat room which is free to join on this link: http://talkback.writers-online.co.uk/, and details of local face to face groups in your district at your local public library, or on the National Association of Writers' Groups website at http://www.nawg.co.uk/. This website features many local and national writing competitions, too.

You could start your own blog using Blogger or Wordpress (a Weebly website includes a blog page), in which you write about your journey towards publication. If you sound friendly and approachable, other writers will want to follow your progress. If you ask published authors for interviews they will almost always oblige. Many interviews on blogs take the form of question and answer sessions – you provide the questions, the author answers them by email, then you post the results on your blog – simple!

Join social networking and fan fiction groups, then you'll meet other authors, published and unpublished, experienced and just starting out, in a friendly and informal setting.

These days blogs and websites are easy to make and manage, even if you have only shoestring funds or no funds at all.

margaretjamesblog.blogspot.co.uk/ is a blog generated from free Blogger software available from Google.

www.creativewritingmatters.co.uk/ uses the Pro version of a Weebly website and is very reasonably priced. It has a few more bells and whistles than the free version, which is still brilliant and easy to use. http://www.weebly.com

If you want to have your own domain name, Weebly can help or check out the availability at www.123-reg.co.uk/. You may have to pay a small annual fee for a domain name.

There are plenty more blog and site providers on the web, either free or for a small sum. www.youtube.com is a great source of help if you get stuck. Type in the name of the software you are using and the chances are a list of short, explanatory videos will come up.

If you don't have much spare time and your computer is a machine of mystery, but you *do* have the financial means and would like a sophisticated online profile, consider paying a professional to arrange this on your behalf. Don't be surprised by the high prices, though. Remember you are paying for both design skills *and* IT expertise.

Self-publishing

There is no question that self-publishing your work can be a viable and sensible alternative to commercial publishing. It might even be your fast track to fame and fortune. The publishing industry has changed considerably in recent years, and it is not unknown (although it's still rare) for a self-published book to be taken on by a major publishing house and be a big hit.

Self-publishing is not the same as vanity-publishing. Vanity publishers make their money from authors, not books, and are in it for the cash they can extort from the gullible, the deluded and – yes – the vain. If you *self*-publish your book, however, you will pay a percentage of your earnings to Amazon or Smashwords and the like, but after that all the profit is yours.

The commercial publishing industry, personified by literary agents and editors, has always been the gatekeeper of quality as far as presentation and indeed everything else is concerned. But, now that everyone can upload their books on to various selling sites, the Internet is flooded with poorly-produced copy. So it's important to get your presentation as perfect as is humanly possible. Mistakes in spelling, grammar and punctuation can result in changes of meaning. Compare *Father Christmas is coming!* with *Father, Christmas is coming!*

Do you want your reader to understand you? If so, hiring a professional copy-editor to check through your final version might be money well spent.

If you don't employ any professionals, ask *several* people who have the appropriate skills to read your manuscript. It is a fact that the subconscious brain can sometimes correct mistakes which are in front of our eyes. At any rate, you certainly won't see all your own mistakes straight away and, if you put your manuscript to one side for a few weeks, then look at it afresh, you will probably be horrified to see how many blunders you previously missed.

Once it's published online, your book will swim around with all the others in the online sea. The statistics for the Amazon UK site alone are astonishing. In the first year of ebook publication, ten thousand titles were uploaded. The last time we looked, the figure was over two and a half million. How are you going to get your book noticed? Look carefully at the uploading information. Make sure your book is tagged and flagged in as many categories as possible. Then promote it on Facebook, Twitter and on your own blog for all you are worth.

Exercise

If you don't already have Twitter and Facebook accounts, open these soon.

Also consider setting up your own website and/or starting your own blog. While you're thinking about it and/or working out how to do it, look at and comment on the posts on other people's blogs, and also follow these blogs.

Then, when you start your own blog, other bloggers will hopefully follow you and comment on what you say. You'll soon be part of the online writing community.

CHAPTER 8

The Bad Stuff

Jealousy
Writer's block
Rejection
Manners

Jealousy

It's great when life is going well. When it's going badly, however, everything is more of a challenge. It's hard to stay positive and optimistic when things are going wrong for you, especially if you have friends in the same life situations who are having a wonderful time.

We all know jealousy is an unattractive and destructive emotion, but it can be hard not to feel jealous of even a good friend who gets the job you wanted while you remain unemployed, announces her engagement to the man of her dreams while you're still trying to get over being dumped yet again, or sells her first short story or novel while you're attempting to be philosophical about your latest rejection.

We're all members of the top species on this planet, and most human beings are competitive. As writers or aspiring writers, we're in a hugely competitive profession in which someone we know is almost always going to be doing better than us. So it's probably best if we can admit to ourselves that yes, we are sometimes jealous of our more successful writing friends.

Then we need to channel this jealousy into trying to do better ourselves, and into concentrating on finding ways to sell or promote our own work so we become better known and more successful.

Mutual support

Many artistic people seem to be (and apparently always have been) unhappy, restless, angry or depressed. It seems to go with the creative territory.

Perhaps, however, perfect happiness is not particularly conducive to creative endeavour? If you have a lovely family, why would you wish to spend your time in the imagined hell of a dysfunctional one? If you are happily married to the love of your life, why would you want to write about people who are thwarted or unlucky in love, and what would you know about it anyway? Maybe *some* trouble and strife actually *need* to be added to the mix of most authors' lives?

You'll almost certainly find that when you are feeling down other writers will be extremely supportive and encouraging. This is because we can *afford* to be supportive and encouraging, as well as because most writers are lovely people who can't help walking in other people's shoes and empathising with their friends.

We writers are in competition with each other, but – unlike many artists and musicians – we hardly ever have to compete for something as specific as a hanging space in a gallery or a place in an orchestra.

Once you have Twitter and Facebook accounts, you will be able to share your good and bad news with your fellow writers. Whenever things go wrong for you, remember there will always be a demand for stories and there will always be room at the top for the next big thing.

Writer's Block

What do you do when you're stuck, blocked, can't find the energy to go on with a story, or think it might be better for your health and sanity if you give up writing completely?

If your writer's block is of the emotional kind, then rest assured, we all feel like that sometimes! **Do it anyway** may sound unfeeling but can often be the way through if the expectation of what you can achieve is realistic. Otherwise, talking it through with someone who understands, going for a walk or writing something unrelated to your work in progress may help.

If your writer's block is as a result of a problem with your plot, you might consider piece of advice we were given recently. *If you're stuck, have someone come in with a gun and shoot somebody*, and we would agree wholeheartedly with that.

We don't mean shoot somebody literally, of course, although if you're writing mystery or crime fiction perhaps you actually *could* put a few rounds into a character's chest. This will certainly stir things up a bit – or a lot!

Otherwise, shooting somebody could consist of:

1- Giving an established character such as your protagonist or antagonist a shock, a challenge, a setback or a surprise.

2 - Weaving a new plot strand into your story.

3 - Creating a new character and giving this person something exciting and/or interesting to do, but also remembering to make sure this something is integral to your story.

4 - Changing the direction of your story by putting in a turning point. Darcy's letter to Elizabeth at the midpoint of *Pride and Prejudice* is a classic and much quoted example of a turning point.

4 - Letting someone who is (or is going to be) important in your story be born, get married or die.

5 - Changing the circumstances of a character's life – making this person richer, poorer, happier, unhappier, more successful, less successful, and letting this change have a knock-on effect throughout the rest of your story.

Do any of these five possibilities work for you?

You could also try putting your work-in-progress to one side and writing something, anything else – a poem, an article, a letter to a newspaper, an email to your best friend.

Where can you find inspiration?

If you have a file full of suggestions, thoughts and jottings, get it out and look through it. If you don't have such a file, start one now. We keep interesting cuttings, photographs, articles and postcards which we hope will inspire us when we've run out of steam, and often they do.

Actually touching or otherwise investigating an inanimate object can be seriously inspirational. A piece of china or porcelain, for example – what does it look like, feel like, what is its history? Who owned it last? Who owns it now?

Maybe you could go to the sort of museum where visitors are encouraged to interact with the exhibits, and have some new experiences there? Maybe you could play a gamelan or try on some period costumes?

Or perhaps you could listen to a piece of music? Movie music, which is written specifically to create a certain mood or even several moods, can be especially inspirational.

If you're writing romantic fiction, an adventure story or heroic fantasy, you could try listening to the music from *The Lord of the Rings* trilogy (Howard Shore) or from *Gladiator* (Hans Zimmer) or almost anything by John Williams – it's all highly motivating stuff.

If you are feeling seriously blocked, to the point where every sentence written is a Herculean task, then try listening to music that is new to you. If you're a popular music fan, try opera – and vice versa. Don't be concerned about whether you like it but do be interested in what makes it work. Think about its rhythm, melody and mood. Imagine people and places. Music is constantly moving. Perhaps journeys come to mind.

In classical music terms the nineteenth century is often referred to as the Romantic period. Composers wrote a lot of 'programme' music which is descriptive and contains a recurring theme. In some ways this is similar to having a main character.
Try listening to:

Rimsky-Korsakov *Scheherazade*
Berlioz *Symphonie Fantastique*
Mendelssohn *Fingal's Cave*
Stravinsky *The Rite of Spring*
Karl Jenkins *The Armed Man*
David Bowie *Space Oddity*

It's very common for one art form to inspire another. In *Appassionata* by Cathie Hartigan http://www.womanandhome.com/news-and-entertainment/295059/appassionata the cor anglais solo in Dvorak's *New World* symphony provided inspiration. In Cathie's story *City Break* http://www.womanandhome.com/news-and-entertainment/435094/city-break it was Raeburn's painting of the Reverend Robert Walker.

Rejection

This is the Big One, the monster, the thing all writers hate, even experienced, established writers, even writers who have told themselves over and over again that rejection is not about them, it's about market forces, it's about the idiosyncratic preferences of editors, it's about the person who wrote the rejection letter suffering from a painful and intimate medical condition and wanting to take it out on somebody.

Does it help to know there can't be many or even any published writers who have never had a rejection of any kind? Or that some now hugely successful writers wear their early rejections as badges of honour and actually laugh about these former setbacks? Or that commissioning editors at major publishing houses have lost their jobs when they've let a big fish swim away?

What doesn't kill me, makes me stronger, as the German philosopher Friedrich Nietzsche, he of the astonishing moustache, is supposed to have said – and which many other people must have said, too.

When you get a rejection, give yourself a few hours to get over the initial shock, outrage, anger or dismay. Then, after you've had a drink, and maybe also something good to eat, reread the message/letter or replay the telephone/face-to-face conversation in your head. It probably wasn't all about you, was it? Or even about your work? It was also about the state of the market, the current trends in publishing, the difficulties of promoting new writing by previously unknown authors. It *is* time-consuming, challenging and expensive for a publisher to launch a new writer, especially a novelist. All commercial print publishers want to see a good return on their investment.

What was actually said?

If you were given any practical advice about your work, think about what was said. Maybe the person giving you this advice is right? Maybe your adventure story *isn't* exciting enough? Maybe your romantic hero *isn't* particularly attractive? Maybe your romantic heroine, who you meant to be sharp and funny, *is* a bitch? Maybe you *do* take too long to get started on your story? Maybe your story, which you meant to end with a triumphant firework display of action and/or emotion, *does* fizzle out? You can do something about any or all of this.

It's never easy to be told you're unwanted and to go away, and maybe in future it won't happen to any authors any more. As the digital revolution gathers pace, we'll all be able to self-publish our work on websites and as electronic downloads, even if we're the least technically-minded people in the world.

The only people we will have to court, cajole and delight will be our readers, and we'll wait in fear and trembling for them to give us their opinions in the form of reviews on public websites which the whole English-speaking world will be able to read.

Nowadays, commercial publishers respect and even court reviews on ordinary readers' websites. It's becoming commonplace for publishers to quote Amazon reviews by ordinary readers in commercially published novels. See, for example, the reviews for Sophie Duffy's second novel *This Holey Life*, published by Legend Press.

As recently as twenty years ago, most writers probably didn't think about their readers very much, or even at all. Their big challenge was to impress a literary agent, a magazine editor or a commercial publisher, and to worry about what readers might think of their work much later in the process.

But these days we have to think about our readers from the outset. This is both comforting and alarming, but we find it mostly comforting. Nowadays, a writer who believes in his or her work can self-publish online, on Amazon, on a blog or on a fan-fiction website, and see what happens next.

———

In the case of E L James, author of the Christian Grey trilogy of novels, quite a lot happened next! The stories were originally published on fan-fiction websites, created a big buzz, and ordinary readers made those books the success they are today.

It will cost you nothing to publish your work on your own website or blog. If readers like your writing, they will read it online, they will tell their friends about it, and one day they might even pay money for the whole book.

We're not in the business of fortune-telling, but it's been suggested by many people in the industry that in future print publishing at the expense of a commercial publishing company could well be restricted to children's and gift books, and maybe even those will go digital in the end.

But, in the meantime, many of us will still have to cope with rejection letters or rejection emails from literary agents, magazine editors and commercial publishers.

Coping with rejection

Do we, the authors of this book, have any practical experience of dealing with rejection?

Yes, indeed we do. So, whenever we receive rejection letters or messages, we work through our **six stage plan**:

1 - We read the letter or email.
2 - We have a good grumble both to ourselves and to our friends.
3 - We screw the letter up and chuck it in the bin or we relegate the email to the delete folder with a nicely satisfying click.
4 - We have a treat – a chocolate éclair or a custard doughnut always hits the spot, so we keep some in the freezer for emergencies like these.
5 - We fish the letter out of the bin or get the email out of the folder.
6 - We read it again to see if it says anything sensible, which actually it might – and, if it does, we resolve to act on the advice, but *not* until we are feeling calmer and more philosophical.

If your short story didn't win a competition or was rejected by a magazine, it might have been because it wasn't the right sort of story, or because you didn't follow the magazine's submission instructions or obey the competition rules.

If your novel was rejected, check to see if you sent it to the right sort of publisher. Mills & Boon publishes only romantic fiction, but this doesn't stop people sending in all kinds of writing – crime, mystery, fantasy and family saga, to name but four kinds of fiction which Mills & Boon definitely *doesn't* publish, at least at the time of writing this book – only to get it straight back again.

Some subjects were fashionable once but aren't fashionable any more. If you're writing about last year's hot new subject, the chances are a publisher will have been swamped by submissions already, and won't want yours. Publishers are always looking for the *next* big thing.

What is the next big thing going to be? This is a very good question, one to which publishers don't always know the answer, so it's a problem for authors and publishers alike.

Publishers were all slow on the uptake in respect of *Fifty Shades of Grey*, probably because most of them believed erotic fiction was still a niche market with a comparatively small reader base. We feel it's likely that the *Fifty Shades*-and-its-many-imitators furore will eventually die down and erotic fiction will become a niche market once again.

Or will it?

Who can tell?

The world of publishing is full of surprises. Who would have thought a story about a boy wizard would make its author one of the richest women of all time?

We feel the best advice we can give is to write what you *want* to write, what makes you happy, and – while you are writing – to keep trying to put yourself in your reader's place and asking yourself: if I were a reader, would I like this?

While you're waiting to see if you've cracked it, next-big-thing-wise, bear in mind that even J K Rowling had to go through a long-winded rejection process before her first Harry Potter novel was snapped up by Bloomsbury. A seven volume story about a boy wizard, scoffed most publishers – that will *never* sell!

A story about rabbits searching for a new home – who wants to read about rabbits? Luckily for Richard Adams and a small independent publisher who believed in him, it turned out that quite a few *million* people wanted to read *Watership Down.*

So have faith in yourself, enjoy the writing process, and with a bit of luck you will make it in the end. If you decide you can't be bothered with the commercial publishing process – and this is what many writers are deciding nowadays– go straight to your readers online at minimal or no cost to yourself.

You'll soon find out what your product consumers – your real, live, human readers – think of your work.

Manners

We'll round off this chapter with some thoughts on manners – the bad sort – for readers *and* writers.

You've probably read a few (or maybe even many) short stories and novels which you've hated? Perhaps you didn't finish them, but you felt very strongly that what you *did* read was a total waste of your time?

Maybe you hated one or two (or even more) so much that you told your friends and family not to read/buy them because you were offended, revolted and/or bored out of your mind?

Perhaps, in the case of a novel, you even fired off a short one star or two star review to Amazon or Goodreads full of emotive words like **rubbish** and **stupid** and **awful**?

What did you say?

Did you try to help the author and the reading public by explaining what you felt was wrong with the book and suggesting how the author could improve?

We hope you did!

But, if you didn't, how do you think *you* would feel if you were on the receiving end of a review which trashed your work *without* saying anything helpful or constructive? A review which was merely gratuitous abuse?

When you become a published author, your literary baby is out there naked and alone in the world. It has no defence against anyone who wants to hurt it. You've read as far as Chapter 8 of this book, so we assume (and we hope) you are planning to join the ranks of published authors some time soon. You know how much effort and emotional energy goes into making a work of fiction. So now, when you find you really dislike the work of another author – and it *will* happen, because we don't all like everything – try to work out *why* you hated it, and perhaps send the author a private message via the author's blog or website, before you go online, spoil that author's day, and maybe suggest to the world that *you* get a kick out of being spiteful?

As for when you are speaking to published authors – **here's a checklist of questions which are likely to rile/upset/dismay any writer**, especially if they are asked in a social group or at a meeting/event/conference rather than in a private conversation.

How much do you earn?
What advance did you get for your last book?
How many books have you sold during your writing life?
Does your husband/wife mind you being a writer?

Do you ever wish you could write like (name one or more of your own favourite authors)?
My son/daughter/husband/wife has written a really good novel, but nobody will publish it. I happen to have it here in my bag. So will you read it and give us your professional opinion?
Why can't I find your books in W H Smith/Waterstones?
Why can't I find your books in charity shops?
Why aren't your books in the bestseller charts?
Do you think you have any chance of winning the Booker Prize?

Here are some questions **authors are almost always happy to answer**:

Do you come from a family of writers?
How long have you been a writer?
Where do you find the inspiration for your stories?
What are you writing now?
Do you enjoy writing and where/how do you find you write best?
What time of day do you write?
Where can I buy your books?
I've brought along one of your books – please will you sign it for me?
What advice would you give someone who wants to be an author?

When you become a commercially published author yourself, here are some things it would be **tactless to ask the reading public** – even or especially if they're what you are really thinking and would like to know!

If you don't like the sort of stuff I write, why are you at this meeting/talk/event?
Sir/madam, have you actually read any of my books?
Why don't you tell this audience what *you* earn?
How successful are you in your *own* career?

Although thousands of books are published annually in the UK alone, the publishing industry is a small one. Readers and writers and publishers and literary agents remember compliments and they also remember insults. We can't always be kind and generous to each other, but in this hothouse industry it's always wise to try.

Exercise

Find a piece of commercially published writing which you absolutely hate and then try to work out *why* you hate it. What's wrong with it, and –

this is much more important – what's right with it?

Okay, it doesn't appeal to you. But why did it appeal to someone else, someone who was prepared to spend their own money producing, publishing and promoting it?

As a writer and communicator, it's not enough to say any writing which you hate is just not your sort of thing. You need to go beyond that and work out why *other* people might like it, even if you don't.

CHAPTER 9

I am a writer

Doing and being
Writing communities
Writing groups
Starting a group
What sort of group?

1 - Are you a creative writing student, or are you a writer, pure and simple?

2 - If someone asks what you do, can you say *I am a writer* without feeling embarrassed or fraudulent?

3 - Do you want writing to be your hobby?

4 - Or do you want writing to be your life?

Each of the four questions above should make you ask yourself if writing is an integral part of your being and is what you need to do in order to make sense of the world? Or if it is just something you do in your spare time.

We're not suggesting writers have to spend their entire lives in front of a screen. How much money they earn doesn't come into the equation. Unfortunately, not all writers make a living solely from their writing. Many supplement their incomes from teaching or part time jobs, or they have supportive parents or partners.

Constantly regarding all our experiences as fodder for our writing is normal for writers. Being curious, obsessing over minutiae and daydreaming about possibilities are all central to the writer's life. In addition to being an artist and a craftsperson, being a searching critic and a staunch fan of your own endeavours is also desirable, while having a sense of humour can be life-saving.

You might think you will always be a student, and to some extent this is the case. We writers are in a profession in which we are always learning. But, after a certain amount of time, success or the completion of a body of work, there may come a shift in consciousness, and being a writer will become your natural state.

Writing communities

We don't mean you have to forsake your family and friends and go to live in a community! But writing can be a lonely and isolating experience. So meeting other writers for tea (or stronger) and sympathy is beneficial even if their opinions don't line up with yours. They do have an understanding of what it means to write.

If you are comfortable about using the Internet (and it's worth becoming comfortable) and/or you can't get to a face-to-face writing group, you may well find an Internet forum to which you could contribute. Somewhere online there will be a forum for every sort of writing you can imagine. Some of these forums are genre or author based, and if you google them you will easily find them. Fan fiction abounds, particularly in Fantasy.

One of the benefits of Internet forums is that you can read the work of a colossal number of people even if you don't contribute a word of your own writing. While this might not be in the spirit of the thing, you can learn a lot from reading a wide variety of work by other creative writers working in all genres.

Many university courses have forums for students to critique each other's work. But we would like to sound a note of caution about receiving and writing critiques on line: it's very easy to click *send*. It isn't so easy to rebuild someone's fragile self-confidence.

You probably don't need to take critiques which feature comments like *I don't read this sort of tripe* and other direct insults to heart. As we suggest in our comments on bad manners in the previous chapter, there is evidence that some strange people get a lot of pleasure from writing malicious critiques whether or not they have actually read the work.

Reading, writing and book groups

Nowadays, almost every city, town or village street boasts a **book group**. If you're a writer, it's a very good plan to belong to one. Apart from the enjoyment you'll get from meeting up to discuss something you enjoy doing, most people find a major benefit is being encouraged to read books they would otherwise shun, or of which they would be unaware. Earlier in this book, we discussed the benefits that reading widely can have on your writing.

A writing group is both like and not like a book group.

Many **writing groups** consist of enthusiastic amateurs, although some contain published authors and some *only* published authors. If you wish to join a writing group it's important to find one which will not only suit you, but will also be happy to have you.

Ask yourself: what do you hope to gain from being in a group?

Useful advice?
Critiquing of your work?
Career advancement?
To tap into the collective imagination?
To socialise with other writers?

Not all groups will be able to provide all these things. You won't need to take much notice of destructive critiques which are obviously based on personal opinions and prejudices (critiques which begin with *I can't say I like stories which feature lots of sex/violence/unusual pets/interplanetary exploration* are always going to be suspect), rather than on an understanding of what you are trying to achieve.

Belonging to a writing group will not automatically further your career unless some of the members know something about the publishing industry. If you find yourself in a group which has members who are commercially published, make sure you listen to what they say.

The atmosphere in a room of writers busily writing is very special. On a good day, it's almost possible to hear the creativity humming. A positive and generous group will share ideas in an atmosphere of respect for each other's efforts.

Being in a group of writers who *write*, as opposed to in a group of writers who merely *talk* about writing is going to matter, unless you are there just for the company and don't mind what you discuss. Writing is an interesting subject, after all. Besides, there might be tea and buns, too.

Consider what you have to offer your group. Apart from your genius, that is. Are you a good listener and able to give a fair critique of someone else's work?

New writers understandably feel daunted by the prospect of joining an established group, but we hope you'll be brave and give it a go. There's a lot to be learned on your writing journey and hardly anyone is confident at the outset. If you join a friendly group, its members will be keen to find and encourage your talent.

Starting a group

If you can't find a group nearby, or your local group is full, or you're not keen on the way this local group operates, consider starting one yourself. If you are a student in a class, you might find you have a ready-made group by the end of the term or year. Or maybe you have friends who are keen to have a go at writing? The fact that someone hasn't written before doesn't mean they can't write at all.

Drawing up an agenda, perhaps spread over the next few months or even a whole year, is a formal way of deciding what topics the group should write about and what else the group might like to do.

Often, someone will suggest a subject or an exercise and the results will be read out at the next meeting. This sort of thing might not be appropriate for every group, especially for those made up primarily of novelists, whose time-frame for completion is long, which means they are often unwilling to read from work in progress.

As for exercises – primary school teachers know the value of subjects like: *My day out* and: *What I had for dinner.* When children write about these things, the teacher gets considerable insights into the lives of the children as well indications of their abilities. For adult writing groups, keeping the exercises simple will do much the same thing. Listening to the host of different ideas that come from the same stimulus is a valuable learning experience.

We're assuming the atmosphere in your group is one of generosity rather than competition. It's okay to think: *I wouldn't have said that.* It's *not* okay to say: *you shouldn't have said that* unless – and this is significant – the writer isn't achieving what he or she set out to achieve, or is making factual or grammatical errors which sabotage their work.

Exercises

All of these would make good exercises for writers of any age.

We have deliberately kept them general in the hope they will encourage a wide variety of responses from individuals or from writing groups as a whole.

If you're in a group, most value is likely to be gained by everyone reading their work out loud. Although it doesn't seem likely, listening to ten pieces of writing about one object can be a more enriching experience than ten pieces about ten objects.

Experiment with how you carry out the exercises below.

Objects

If we asked you to write about a desk, where would you begin? With your own school or work desk? A desk you would like? What's in or on the desk? Where is the desk? Whose desk is it? The writing riches one can mine from objects are dependent on the questions you ask about them.

Consider writing about any of the following objects:

The desk (or any piece of furniture)
The cup
The key(s)
The carrier bag (or any sort of bag)

Characters from objects

Let's approach a character from an oblique perspective. Clothes say a lot about us. Think of a specific person's coat. What sort of coat is it? Old or new? From a charity shop or a designer boutique? Who does the coat belong to? What's in the pockets? How would someone feel in that coat? What would the coat say about them? Writers need to be chronically curious about every aspect of human beings – their mannerisms, their foibles, their hopes, their fears, their dress sense.

Consider writing about the owner of:

A bomber jacket
A mink coat
A blazer
A cape

Characters from occupations

What we do in our lives has a direct bearing on who we are. Think about the following occupations and, while avoiding stereotypes – Tom is rather tall to be an astronaut, after all – can you write about the following characters?

A Big Issue seller
An astronaut – hello, Tom!

A Hollywood star
A dentist

Dialogue

How a person speaks may reveal more about them than *what* they say. Check that your characters have their own voices and don't all sound like you. Consider age, origin and, especially in Britain, class. Peer groups and professions often have their own vocabulary and jargon.

Consider writing some dialogue inspired by the settings/situations below:

Two strangers stuck in a lift
The waiting room
The audition
The laundrette

Tension

Every story contains (or should contain) some tension. It's the thing that pulls us through. We catch hold of the thread on the first page, then find we can't let go. Tension makes our imaginations create entire worlds. It makes the hairs on the backs of our necks stand up and our hearts beat faster. Will they/won't they – that's what we ask ourselves.

Consider writing a scene which features:

Escape
The race
A natural disaster
The secret

Themes

Tension needs fuel. Why are the lovers/brothers/children running away? Why does she want to kill/marry him? Something has to motivate your characters.

Consider writing about:

Betrayal
Passion
Ambition
Revenge

Exercises to do together

Everyone sits in a circle. In the middle is a ball of wool. The first person to pick it up begins to tell a story. After a minute or two, this person throws the ball to someone else while still keeping hold of one end of the wool.

The new person holding the ball carries on with the story. Gradually, the middle of the circle becomes a woolly star, then a cat's cradle, until the story draws to a close – hopefully before too many knots have been formed.

Doing this is fun and, if you're in a group of like-minded writers, an almost credible story can emerge from it. Crucially, it's a *told* story as opposed to *written* one. Our experience of written chain stories is that they usually end up as unlikely tales full curious tangents, deliberate diversions and differing writing styles. Again, they can be fun to write, but not that productive for the individual.

There are other exercises that require the participation of everyone and can be useful as well as enjoyable:

The story generator

This requires a chart the size of a landscape A4 sheet of paper with four columns, and between six and ten rows. The headings for each row are:

Who? (A character's name, age and occupation)

What do they want? (This can be a life ambition or a small desire)
What's the problem? (Or obstacle they must overcome to achieve their ambition)
How do they overcome it?

The best way of filling in the chart is to *keep passing it round* having written in just *one* box. Go *down* each column before starting the next.

Eventually, the whole chart is complete and it is possible to see a simple story outline emerge by reading across a row. Here is an actual example generated by a class:

Who?	What do they want?	What's the problem?	How is it overcome?
Katherine 46 vet	To win X-Factor	She's not that good a singer or anything else	She trains her pet duck to perform with her
Tami 21 cashier in betting shop	To go to Las Vegas	She's not got enough money	She fiddles the till
Carlos 23 waiter	To become a lorry driver with a full HGV licence	He is an illegal immigrant	He looks for a UK bride

Bruce 20 bungee jump instructor	To impress girlfriend with his cooking	She likes Pot Noodles	In bed
Brian 48 carpenter	To climb Everest	He is in a wheelchair	Learns to walk with blades. It's a start!
Andrea 39 museum curator	To get together with John, the Head Archivist	His wife	Locks the wife in sarcophagus
Donald 57 captain of industry	To take over the competition	He is facing fraud charges	Escapes to country outside extradition treaty

Other storylines may be generated by drawing a line that *doesn't* go straight across but *zig-zags* through the columns. Although not obvious to begin with, *the most interesting and unusual stories come from reading across in this way.* The trick is to make them credible even though at first glance they may be preposterous. It isn't necessary to stick exactly to the brief. Andrea can become Andrew very easily if that makes for a better story. He might not be a curator; he could be on holiday in Egypt. It isn't cheating if another idea comes along that inspires you. This sort of exercise is about lighting the imaginative flame.

Consequences

Many people have played this as a party game. Like the story generator, the paper is passed round but in Consequences each line written is folded over and hidden from the sight of the next player. Part of the enjoyment is pairing Napoleon with Cleopatra and discovering they met on the London Eye.

For writing groups, avoiding the use of historical figures or contemporary celebrities and introducing some conflict or difficulty in step 7 usually produce a viable (with a few tweaks) storyline. Here is a version suitable for a class or group:

1 - Name plus age and occupation
2 - Another name etc
3 - Met at...
4 - One said (a problem?)
5 - The other replied (some advice?)
6 - So they went...
7 - What went wrong...
8 - The consequence was...

Speed dating (not exactly)

This is a very useful exercise for clarification of a story or for talking through difficulties.

The group divides into pairs. One person stays put throughout the exercise and the other person moves around the room.

One person tells the other about the story or piece he or she is writing, outlining the characters and plot in a few sentences. The other person then asks relevant questions such as those mentioned in Chapter 5:

How old and from what social class or educational background is your ideal reader?
What sort of story is it – action-packed, reflective, philosophical, simple, complex?
When and where is it set?
Whose story is it?
If you were to sum up your main character in two or three words, what would they be?
Do you need every character?
Is it wise to name your characters Ted, Ed and Ned or Joan, Jane and Jan? Consider Alex, Sam and Chris carefully, too – male or female?
What problems do the characters face?
What attributes do they reveal in trying to overcome them?

What are you going to hold back from revealing, so the reader keeps reading in order to find out what it could be?
What does the main character learn/realise/overcome by the end?
What has changed by the end of your story?

An acute listener will pick up where the writer is hazy or confused and flag this up. It's a good plan to take notes. After swapping roles, the 'stayer' then moves on and the process is repeated. Different pairings reveal different aspects of the writing needing attention.

If everyone says the same negative things, it's probable there's an issue with the writing.

Don't be surprised if there is a lot of waffling the first time you try this. Both writers and listeners will improve with practice. Gradually, the waffling will diminish, to be replaced by tightly-focused questions and answers – we hope!

Being able to talk about your work clearly *and concisely* is an important skill. Remember that the first thing you will be asked when you say you have written a story is: what's it about? Most people don't want a ten thousand word reply.

What sort of group?

Think carefully about what sort of group you want. Exeter Writers, our own local group, has twenty-five members, a committee of six, an annual agenda, a bank account and a website. It holds fortnightly meetings in a church hall and runs an annual, open short story competition.

Other small groups meet at intervals in each other's houses solely to share work, and there is no bureaucracy involved at all.

You could also meet in a pub, in a local community centre, in a library or in a school. If you have to hire a venue, money is going to be an issue. What's the minimum number of members you will need if the group is to be sustainable? What's the maximum the room can hold? How many people should you have in your group if people are to be able to read their work aloud without those in the queue behind them breathing down their necks and getting restless?

CHAPTER 10

Making Some Money

Short stories
Competitions
Articles

Most people who are new to writing fiction find themselves drawn to short stories, probably because they are short. A short story isn't going to be anything like as big an investment of time, energy and emotion as a novel, so it seems an attractive proposition. Or at least not a daunting one.

Authors also wonder if it might be possible to earn some actual *money* from writing short stories.

The good news is – yes, it's certainly possible, and writing short fiction has been a stepping stone for many authors who have then gone on to write novels.

These days, lots of people are putting their collections of short stories up on Amazon Kindle and on other websites such as Smashwords. Some of these ebook collections are selling very well.

Commercial publishers have noticed, and they're getting in on the act, too – asking their authors to contribute to collections of short stories which will hopefully encourage readers to buy their novels, too.

The bad news is – the most lucrative markets for short stories, which in the UK are women's magazines (these pay between about £50 to £300, or more if you are a bestselling/celebrity author, for a 1,000 – 3,000 word short story) and national and local radio stations, have contracted considerably in recent years. It's almost impossible to interest a commercial publisher in a collection of short stories, even though some very talented authors do manage it – for example, the young Nepalese writer Prajwal Parajuly, whose debut from Quercus is a collection of short stories entitled *The Gurkha's Daughter*.

As for novels – you get paid what other people think you are worth, and it's not really possible to suggest how much this might be. A commercial publisher will probably offer you an advance against royalties, but this will be negotiable, and you won't earn anything more until you have earned out this advance. If you're self-published, your income will directly reflect your sales.

A novelist whose work appears as printed volumes can also earn respectable sums of money from the sale of subsidiary rights – large print, audio, foreign/translation and digital – and from Public Lending Right, for which authors have to apply: https://www.plr.uk.com.

But don't despair because another market has expanded, looks set to go on expanding forever, and this market is – competitions. Online and postal competitions are thriving, with new ones cropping up almost every day.

Many of these competitions are for short fiction and have entry fees, which pay for the cash prizes.

What, you have to pay people to read your work?

Yes, we're afraid so. But perhaps you could view entering competitions as you would view making a small investment on which you *hope* to make a return, while not *depending* on it.

At first, you might not win anything much. Or anything at all. But – as time goes on and as you develop your story-telling skills – you should start getting longlisted, then shortlisted, then winning runner-up prizes, and finally some third, second or even first prizes, too.

Our tip is to look for new competitions and small, local competitions with relatively modest prizes, and gradually to work your way up to short story competitions such as the Bridport – http://www.bridportprize.org.uk/ – and the Fish – http://www.fishpublishing.com/ – international competitions which attract literally thousands and thousands of entries. So everyone's chances of winning the Bridport and the Fish are always going to be slim, however brilliant their stories might be.

There are competitions for novelists, too, run by various local authorities, by private individuals and societies, and by publishing houses. If you do some googling, you will find them easily. CreativeWritingMatters organises and administers the Exeter Novel Prize, which was first awarded in March 2014. See www.creativewritingmatters.co.uk for details.

Although this book is intended for creative writing students – that is, for writers of fiction, for people who make things up – we feel we should talk a little about writing non-fiction, too.

This is because people who write non-fiction also tell stories, and because for many writers the road to paid employment is paved with commissions from magazines, newspapers and small publishers who are sometimes willing to pay freelances to write for them.

We say *sometimes* because local newspapers don't always pay freelances for stories. But, if you want to start a cuttings collection of your published work, featuring those all-important bylines which get your name in print, your local paper might offer you some great openings, and – in due course – maybe even a paid column every week.

A non-fiction article for a magazine or newspaper is or ought to be a story:

which is true, and
which can be open-ended – you might not know
what happens next, but this won't matter if you
can follow up events and report back to your
readers later the same day/week/month/year,
and
which is about something interesting, unusual,
cheering, sensational or astonishing.

If you're writing non-fiction, what you write *has* to be true, and you'll risk getting into serious trouble if you embellish, fabricate or lie in print. You could even end up in court being prosecuted for defamation or libel and, if this happens, don't assume the magazine or newspaper will automatically stick up for you.

So – if in doubt, leave it out.

If you interview or quote someone, try to be sure you reproduce what this person actually said, as opposed to what you think or wish he or she said. People can get very upset if they're misquoted. When you're writing your article and quoting your interviewee, don't make a habit of doing anything more radical than ironing out a strong regional accent – *I done it like her told me* can be replaced with *I did what she told me* – and correcting the person's grammar.

A non-fiction writer starts from the same vantage point as the short story writer or novelist in that he or she describes places, machinery, architecture or situations in relation to the human beings who see them, use them, live in them or experience them. Although non-fiction writers can write about animals, aeroplanes and landscapes, as well as about people, they usually tie these stories to the human beings who've also been involved:

Man of 105 pilots Spitfire over Solihull.
Year 7 schoolgirl becomes online millionairess.

Famous novelist's parrot passes Key Stage 1 in English.

You article or news item will need to explain:

Whose story you are telling.
What this person or animal did.
What went right.
What went wrong.
What happened in the end – if you know!

Journalists, novelists, dramatists – they all tell stories.

If you would like to try writing interviews, start off by asking some authors, because authors are always anxious to promote their work, and are usually more than happy to talk about themselves.

You don't *have* to be working for a magazine or newspaper because you could post these interviews on your own blog. You could also start a book review forum. Once you have some followers – get your friends and family to sign up – many publishers will send you review copies of books, and in no time at all you'll have a free library.

Questions you could ask a writer include:

Why did you decide to become a writer?
How did you go about achieving your ambition?
Who or what helped you to succeed, and did you have any lucky breaks?
Who or what hindered you, and what setbacks did you have to overcome?
Who or what inspired you to write your most recently published book?
What advice would you give someone who wants to be a writer?

You can think about answers to these questions for when you are interviewed yourself.

If you're not yet confident you can do any of the above, but you would like to receive a small payment for your writing once in a while, you could try sending off tips, hints, letters, short factual items and stories about your real life experiences to newspapers and magazines. When you start to get paid for these, your confidence will increase, and soon you'll feel ready to tackle articles and short stories.

Exercise

Practise communicating with strangers, a skill which all writers need to master, by interviewing someone you've never met before. We've found that if you tell almost anyone you are writing a book, they will be happy to talk to you.

Or, if that's too daunting, interview a friend or a relative. Or interview yourself. Or you could interview a character in one of your stories. There's quite a fashion for this right now – see http://www.bookbabe.blogspot.co.uk/2012/04/penny-bangle-blog-tourgiveawayreview.html#.UJGflW8xqT4.

CHAPTER 11

Readers of novels – what do they want?

Mostly, they want:

Romantic fiction
Women's-interest fiction
Historical fiction
Crime novels
Thrillers
Mysteries
Adventure stories
Fantasy
Science fiction
Literary fiction

Who is your reader?

Romantic fiction is read mostly by women. A romantic novel usually tells the story of an emotional (but not necessarily sexual) relationship between two people who fall in love. The narrative trajectory of a romantic novel tends to be – the lovers meet, the lovers part or are separated or disagree for some reason, the lovers are reunited. The RNA's (Romantic Novelists' Association's) website – www.rna-uk.org – is a mine of information for both readers and writers. Bestselling authors include Jenny Colgan, Carole Matthews, Trisha Ashley.

Women's-interest fiction is often family-oriented and discusses issues such as adoption, divorce, domestic violence, child-rearing. Most of its authors are female, as are most of its readers. Many writers of women's-interest fiction belong to the RNA, the RWA (Romance Writers of America), or similar organisations around the world. Bestselling authors include Joanna Trollope, Rowan Coleman, Diane Chamberlain.

Historical fiction is of course set in the past. The Historical Novel Society's website states that *to be deemed historical (in our sense), a novel must have been written at least fifty years after the events described, or have been written by someone who was not alive at the time of those events (who therefore approaches them only by research).* See the Society's website for more details – http://historicalnovelsociety.org/. Bestselling authors include Bernard Cornwell, C J Sansom, Maureen Lee.

Crime novels, **thrillers** and **mysteries** all ask the question: who did something, and why? This something doesn't always have to be a murder. Although there are thousands of successful male writers of crime, thriller and mystery fiction, there are also thousands of successful female crime, thriller and mystery writers, and many female readers love these genres. The Crime Writers' Association's website is a useful resource – www.thecwa.co.uk. Bestselling authors include Stuart MacBride, Ruth Rendell, Val McDermid.

Adventure stories are often about seeking lost cities full of treasure, sunken ships full of treasure, journeying in inhospitable places and/or finding yourself by putting yourself through a lot of discomfort and tribulation. Bestselling authors include David Gibbins, Scott Mariani and Raymond Khoury.

Fantasy and science fiction are read by both men and women with men perhaps predominating, especially in the case of science fiction. Readers and writers tend to find each other through fan sites such as http://www.theonering.net/. Bestselling authors include George R R Martin, Mark Lawrence, Robin Hobb.

Literary fiction – what is it? If you ask twenty people, you'll probably get twenty different answers. It is – or most of the people who write it and describe themselves as literary novelists seem to hope or intend it to be – beautifully written in elegant, expressive, emotive language, making full use of the resources of the language. In much literary fiction, style seems to be as important as substance. It often asks the big questions – why do we exist, what are our duties to the planet, to ourselves and to our gods, does capital punishment deter anyone? What exactly *is* human nature? There are no dedicated associations specifically for literary novelists. If you feel you are or want to be a literary novelist, these links might give you food for thought: http://litreactor.com/columns/storyville-what-is-literary-fiction and http://www.matthaig.com/30-things-to-tell-a-book-snob-revisited/.

There are of course many other smaller genres and subgenres of fiction – **horror**, **erotica**, **ménage** and **Western**, to name but four.

In this handbook, we do not have the space to cover writing in all adult genres, or writing for children and young adults. But here are some websites you might like to access if *you* wish to write for these specialised markets:

Horror - http://horror.fictionfactor.com/

Erotica -
http://www.filamentmagazine.com/2011/04/nine
-ways-to-write-better-erotic-fiction/
Ménage -
http://kpiet.wordpress.com/2012/08/27/biphobia-
vs-bisexuality/
Western - http://www.wikihow.com/Write-a-
Western-Novel
Children's -
http://greenhouseliterary.com/index.php/site/to
p_tips
Young Adult - http://www.dummies.com/how-
to/content/writing-young-adult-fiction-for-
dummies-cheat-shee.html.

Whatever kind of fiction you are writing, we
hope the notes in this chapter will be useful to
you because – after all – much fiction contains
elements of crime, of mystery, of romance. Many
investigators in crime fiction fall in love, while
husband-and-wife or girlfriend-and-boyfriend
teams solve mysteries.

How do you find your ideal reader, and – if you want to please

this reader – what should you write?

If you intend to self-publish your work, either as a printed book or as an electronic download, you can write whatever you like. Publishers aren't always right, and these days self-published books often do very well indeed, sometimes after their authors have spent months or even years sending their work out, only to have it rejected by commercial publishers again and again for all kinds of reasons, including *there is no market for this kind of story*.

If you're writing a novel, literary agents and commercial publishers are usually very wary of stories which are a blend of several genres because the received publishing wisdom is that the reading public doesn't like these books. This is not necessarily the case, because many self-published novels on Kindle are selling by the thousand to readers who don't care if a novel is a blend of romance *and* crime *and* mystery, provided it's an engaging read which tells a good story.

But it's not usually a good plan to spread your bets by mixing and matching *too* many genres in a single novel: see our example of the kind of submission letter to a literary agent or publisher which you should *never* write below.

If you have confidence in your writing, and you are able to produce a finished book which can be uploaded on to Kindle and Smashwords and so on without any problems, you might decide to cut out the middleman and go straight to your readers.

But, if you want to go down the traditional route to publication and to find a commercial publisher who is prepared to publish your book at his or her own expense, you'll have to be a team player and be prepared to take direction from editors, who might ask you to make fairly radical changes to your work. The end result should be a well-designed and marketable printed or digital book which will be stocked by all the independent booksellers, by all the major high street chains and in all the online bookstores.

Or that's the theory, anyway.

A commercial publisher will pay for production, publicity, marketing, warehousing and distribution, which are prohibitively expensive for many of us. Also, you are perhaps more likely to be taken seriously as an author if someone pays you to publish your book. But, as the digital revolution looks set to change everything about the publishing industry, this might not be the case for very much longer.

All the same, you still need to be aware of the major genres in commercially published fiction. This is because even if you intend to bypass commercial publishers and to self-publish your work, it will still be useful to think about where you will fit into the great scheme of publishing things and about how you can best market your work to your readers.

Literary agents, publishers, editors – do you need them?

What do they do?

They would say they provide the reading public with some guarantee of quality control, and also ensure good books continue to appear in the marketplace.

A literary agent places an author's work with a publisher in exchange for a percentage of the author's gross earnings, which in practice is usually between 10% and 15% of the author's royalties, and usually plus VAT. He or she can be a self-employed sole trader, an employee of an international conglomerate, or something in between.

It is not an agent's job to teach you how to write, but many agents are former editors who are prepared to offer editorial advice, and some will spend a lot of time, money and energy nurturing a promising writer.

You cannot insist on an agent nurturing you, however, because an agent doesn't make any money until he or she sells your work and collects a percentage of your earnings.

Anyone can set up in business as a literary agent. So, if you are looking for one, try to find out who he or she already represents, and if these writers are successfully published – or not.

A literary agent should never charge a fee upfront. Members of the UK's Association of Authors' Agents – see http://www.agentsassoc.co.uk/ to track them down – would hopefully never do this. So don't be tempted to sign up with an agent who asks you for a reading fee, a consultation fee, or any other sort of fee, because all this particular agent wants to do is separate you from your money.

A literary agent owes it to himself or herself to represent authors whose work he or she can sell to publishers, and to turn any other authors away. This is why it is often harder to find an agent than to find a publisher. But don't pity the poor agent, who will make sure he or she takes a percentage plus VAT of any royalties when the author's books are eventually sold.

A publisher bears the whole cost of producing the book, electronic download or whatever form the work of the author takes. He or she will offer the author a **contract** which is a **legally binding document**. So you will need to read a contract carefully, discuss anything with which you don't agree, and clarify any points which you don't understand, well before you sign. If you have an agent, vetting and possibly re-negotiating a contract is something he or she will do for you.

If they don't have literary agents, UK-based writers should join the UK's Society of Authors – see http://www.societyofauthors.org/ – whose experts will vet their contracts for them and offer them sound professional advice.

_____

Editors and **copy-editors** are employed directly by publishers and are on a specific publisher's payroll, or they sell their services to one or more publishers as self-employed freelances. It's their job to make your work look as professional as possible and also to make sure it is the kind of work the publisher wishes to sell.

If becoming a commercially published novelist or other kind of writer is your life's ambition, your submission letter or email to a literary agent or publisher might be the one of the most important you will ever write.

A good submission letter does four key things:

1 - Tells the recipient a little about the book.
2 - Tells the recipient a little about the author.
3 - Makes the recipient want to read the book.
4 - Makes the recipient want to work with the author.

Let's look at a submission letter which gets almost everything wrong.

42 Tripe Street
Bletheridge (1)

Hi Andy (2)

I'm sending you the manuscript (3) of my novel *The Gnomes of Sidmouth*, which is about 200,000 words long. (4)

It's a romantic comedy in which aliens land on earth and a robot falls in love with a beautiful elf in a megalopolis of the future loosely based on a small seaside resort in Devon. The story begins when a town councillor is found dead on a park bench with a bullet through his skull, and later there is some girl-on-girl action, too. (5)

You won't want to miss this opportunity, so why don't I come up to London soonest, meet you for lunch, and we could discuss terms? (6) When you've had a chance to look at the book, I'm sure you'll agree it's destined to become a worldwide bestseller, and you'd be crazy to let it slip through your fingers! (7)

I'm enclosing a photograph of me and my girlfriend on holiday in Ibiza. You can see I'm pretty fit and would look good on a book jacket. (8)

Looking forward to hearing from you, mate!

Cheers

Dave Dumpden

1 - Always give an agent or publisher your full contact details, including phone numbers and email, Twitter and/or Facebook addresses. You need to date your letter and write out the address of the recipient in full, because this is standard business letter procedure, and you're writing – a business letter.

2 - You should address the recipient formally as Dear Mr (or whatever) Surname, unless of course you already know this person and are on cordial terms.

3 - No agent or publisher reads manuscripts (that is, handwritten documents) these days. When you first approach an agent or publisher, you should not send in the whole novel – instead, send a short synopsis (about 500 words maximum) and the first two or three chapters (about 15,000 words).

4 - This is probably too long for a first novel. A print version would be hugely expensive to produce, store in a warehouse and distribute, and it would take up a disproportionate amount of space on a bookshop's shelves. A good length for a first novel would be about 80,000 – 100,000 words, which would become a paperback of about 300 printed pages.

5 - This novel looks as if it's an uneasy mix of almost all popular genres – romance, comedy, science fiction, fantasy, crime, erotica – so it would probably be quite difficult to sell to

booksellers, who might insist the book-buying public wouldn't like it, so they didn't want to stock it.

6 - This sounds too confident and assertive. At this stage, you are courting the agent or publisher and trying to interest him or her in a new writer's work, which might indeed be wonderful, but which might have no commercial value at all.

7 - Again, this sounds too presumptuous, even if it's supposed to be ironic. The use of the cliché about the work slipping through the reader's fingers doesn't promise original, exciting writing.

8 - Contrary to what we are sometimes led to suppose, agents and publishers seeking new writers are more interested in competent writing than in good looks. So, although good looks are a bonus, they won't help if you can't write. Also, it's too soon to be sending agents or publishers your photograph. They won't want a photograph until they sign you up, and maybe not even then.

This letter doesn't tell the recipient anything much – or at least, much that is relevant – about the author. While you don't need to tell a literary agent or publisher your entire life history, you do need to give him or her a *few* relevant facts. Then, he or she can start to build up an image of you. What do you do for a living, roughly how old are you (in your twenties, fifties, eighties), do you have any relevant qualifications – for example, are you perhaps an accountant writing a thriller about a huge financial fraud which is likely to bring down the government?

There's no SAE enclosed for the return of the submission. Of course, we all hope our submissions won't be returned, but it's still good manners to enclose return postage.

This is a much more appealing submission letter:

Nicholas Armitage
34 Bellstone Court
Salutation Walk
Feltingbridge
FT35 7QZ

Tel 02965 945034
Mobile 06845956435
Email nick@hollyberry.co.uk
www.twitter.com/nickbonedigger

13 January 2014

Mr Andrew Barley
Barley and Rye Literary Agency
Renton Mews
London SE45 9TZ

Dear Mr Barley

The Sleep Walkers

I'm sending you the synopsis and first three chapters of my crime novel *The Sleep Walkers*, which is 100,000 words long and is the first in a police procedural series featuring maverick Detective Sergeant Mick Lewinsky of the Devon and Cornwall Constabulary.

Thirty years old, working class and a practising Roman Catholic, Mick is of Irish and Polish stock and is the first member of his family to become a policeman. In *The Sleep Walkers*, he and his boss, the curmudgeonly, golf-loving and soon-to-be-retired Detective Inspector Courtenay, investigate the disappearance of a child from a holiday camp, find a child's body washed up on a beach, and begin a murder enquiry.

But, two days later, the body vanishes from the mortuary. The child turns up alive. A woman throws herself on to a funeral pyre which she has built and lit on the beach where the child's body was found.

At present I am working as a refuse collector, but I also have a first class honours degree in archaeology from the University of Feltingbridge. At university I specialised in osteology, which is the study of bones found at archaeological sites. I am twenty-six and live in a rented flat with my partner Lucy and our two dogs. My parents live in Cornwall, where I grew up and to which I frequently return.

I am a huge fan of crime fiction and would like to become a full time crime novelist myself. I hope my story will appeal to readers who love the work of Ian Rankin, Mark Billingham and Jo Nesbø.

Thank you for considering my work, which I hope you will enjoy reading. If you would like to see more of the novel, I can send you the complete typescript by post or email.

I look forward to hearing from you.

All best wishes

Nicholas Armitage

Enc: Synopsis and first three chapters of *The Sleep Walkers*
SAE

These days, some literary agents and publishers ask authors to submit everything by email. Generally, the submission letter will need to be in the body of the email and anything else will need to be in one or several attachments.

If you're asked to submit in this way, you should still write your email message in conventional English using conventional punctuation, capitalisation and paragraphing. Remember to capitalise the personal pronoun I!

Always follow submission procedures precisely – don't give the publisher an excuse to delete your message unread.

Your synopsis is an important selling tool, and some agents and publishers will read this before they turn to your opening chapters. So try to do these three things:

1- Make it short – 500 words maximum
2 - Make it clear – write in the third person and the present tense, outlining *whose* story you are telling, *where* it is set, *when* it is set, *what* the big question is going to be, and *how* everything is resolved at the end
3 - Make it complete – provide the reader with an outline of the *whole* story

Here is an example of a synopsis of a novel which does all three of those things:

Synopsis
Margaret James
THE PENNY BANGLE

The third and final novel in the Denham family saga, this story begins in 1942 and is set in Dorset, London, Italy and Egypt.

When should you trust your heart?

When nineteen-year-old munitions worker **Cassie Taylor** leaves Birmingham to become a land girl in Dorset, she expects she will be in for a quiet and boring time. But, on arriving at the Denham family's farm, she meets **Robert** and **Stephen Denham**, army officer twins still convalescing after being wounded at Dunkirk.

Although she is initially drawn to lively, friendly Stephen, Cassie falls in love with his brother Robert. When Robert returns to active service, Cassie joins the ATS, not only because she wants to have adventures of her own, but also because she wants to be worthy of Robert. When Cassie meets Robert again in Alexandria, he asks her to marry him. They become engaged but, as the Allies prepare for the invasion of Italy in 1943, Cassie is sent back to England.

Stephen is too unfit to go back on active service and is offered a desk job in London. Stephen is in love with Cassie and, when Robert is declared missing in action, he assumes he can take Robert's place in Cassie's heart. Cassie explains that nobody could ever take Robert's place. But

Stephen assumes that Cassie despises him because he is not a hero.

In Italy, Robert is wounded on a mission behind enemy lines and ends up fighting with the partisans, having been rescued from almost certain death by **Sofia Corelli**. Robert and Sofia become lovers.

In an attempt to prove to Cassie that he is as brave as Robert, Stephen is killed. When Robert is repatriated at the end of the war, he confesses his affair with Sofia to Cassie, assuming she will understand and forgive him.

But Cassie is heartbroken. She tells Robert that their engagement is off, and that she now wishes she had had an affair with Stephen, who might still be alive if she had pretended that she loved him.

Robert is determined to win Cassie back. She is just as determined that she will never marry him. But family circumstances bring them back together, and they finally admit that they both need healing and forgiveness. They marry and the story ends in Dorset as Cassie gives birth to Robert's daughter, Lily Rose.

What about your actual novel?

If you're making a **postal** submission in the UK, the first three chapters of your novel should:

1 - Be typed on good quality A4 paper in 12 point Arial, Times Roman or another clear font such as Bookman, in double spacing with wide margins and with the pages consecutively numbered – don't start each new chapter with the number 1.

2 - Introduce the central character(s) and start telling the story from his/her/their point(s) of view.

3 - Be full of questions to which the reader will want answers.

4 - End with a cliffhanger of some kind.

If you're making an **electronic** submission, the same advice applies. But, before you click *send*, double-check the publisher's guidelines to see if attachments are acceptable. Check the file type too. Don't send your submission as a .doc file if the publisher only accepts .pdf. Sometimes attachments aren't acceptable and you may have to send everything in the body of an email.

What sort of cover will I get and does it matter?

Many commercially-published authors write with an ideal reader in mind. So cover art (and even Kindle editions need cover art to act as their shop windows) will be designed to appeal to these ideal readers.

Here are some examples of standard/traditional cover art:

Romantic comedies often have **cartoon** covers, frequently with a lot of **pink** or **light blue** in them.

Crime novels often have covers done in **neutral** colours, or with some **black** in them, or with an alarming splash of **red**.

Fantasy novels often feature illustrations of **heroes in leggings and tunics** and/or **heroines in mediaeval-style gowns**, standing in front of landscapes full of **castles** and **dragons**.

Our fictitious Nicholas Armitage, whose letter to a literary agent we quoted above, knows where his ideal readers might be found.

Where will you fit in?

Exercise

When you're writing a novel, think about who might want to read it – someone old, someone young, someone male, someone female, someone well-educated, someone who left school with no qualifications at all but who loves good stories?

Then, when you have decided, write a few key scenes with this reader in mind.

Actors sometimes say that at each live performance they choose a member of the audience and then play to this one particular person, rather than to the whole auditorium.

You could perhaps do something similar – write for your ideal reader, rather than mankind in general.

Then you should stay focused on what you want to do.

CHAPTER 12

The roads more or less travelled

Why go on a course?
Where are you?
What course?
What? No course?

The observation below, often attributed to Ernest Hemingway, is repeated over and over in conversations about the teaching of creative writing: *There is nothing to writing. All you do is sit down at a typewriter and bleed.*

Whoever said that knew what he/she was talking about, didn't he/she? So why go on a course?

If you wish to write fiction, but have never written anything apart from emails to friends and family or reports for work, having some sort of creative writing training is probably essential, despite what Mr Hemingway might or might not have said. There will always be those blessed few whose writing arrives fully formed on the page, but they *are* blessed and they are indeed few. In fact, the wise amongst them would probably go on a course anyway, for there is much to be learned about what to do *after* the words are written down.

Most writers find themselves sailing into the doldrums now and again. Perhaps they're stuck for ideas. That first flush of inspiration, which led them to write half a novel or several short stories, has fizzled out. They find they are writing the same story again and again.

If this happens to you, you might feel you want to move outside your comfort zone. But you won't know in which direction to go. The many hours you've spent in an imaginary world have become isolating. You feel the need for company. Maybe you are sociable and your writing is highly regarded by those who know you, but you aren't getting any joy when it comes to publication. You brood.

Who are you?

Although researching courses on Google or at your local library is essential, you'll probably end up feeling the choice is bewildering. A good deal of self-reflection is advisable before committing yourself to one course in particular.

It's important to think hard about what is going on in your life. Don't be distracted by wishing it was somehow otherwise or by wishing you were someone else. Writing requires a lot of enthusiasm, energy and hard work. Here's a list of ten questions you could ask yourself:

1 - Do I hope to earn a living from writing?
2 - Do I want to make a financial investment in my writing?
3 - Writing is something I really enjoy and in which I want to excel, but do I see it as a profession?
4 - Do I like new writing challenges or do I want to specialise in what I enjoy?
5 - Are qualifications important to me?
6 - Do I work well under pressure?
7 - How much time do I have in which to write?
8 - Do I have plenty of self-motivation or do I prefer to have a route laid out before me?
9 - What am I aiming to achieve in five years?
10 - Can I plot the steps I need to take in order to achieve that aim?

Depending on how you answer these questions, a picture may emerge of your way forward.

What course?

Over the last couple of decades, creative writing has become increasingly popular. In 1970 the University of East Anglia offered a post-graduate Master of Arts (MA) course. Ian McEwan was the only student that first year, and his anecdotes about the relaxed atmosphere and tutorials over pints of beer are famous. Now nearly every university and college in the UK is bursting with creative writing courses at every level.

There are also a myriad author-led workshops, writing holidays, correspondence courses and one-to-one critiquing services. Agencies such as www.literatureworks.org.uk, www.spreadtheword.org.uk and www.nawe.co.uk run career development days.

Think about your writing and decide at what level you want to enter a course or career development path. If you aren't sure, then seek guidance. If you are enrolling for an evening class or college course, ask either to speak to the tutor or to have a piece of work assessed. But don't be downhearted if this work comes back with a recommendation that you should take a beginners' class. To put it bluntly, you don't know what you don't know. Besides, if you are passionate about your work, you will be keen to learn as much as possible. It has been known for students to enrol for beginners' classes several times, often repeating exercises. In much the same way as Monet painted his beloved water lilies again and again, seeking different manifestations of light and shadow, so it can be with writing. In any group your writing should be assessed on its own merits.

It is now possible to take Creative Writing as a single subject at undergraduate degree level. There is usually a choice of modules for specialisation, such as prose, poetry, screen and scriptwriting. A dissertation is normally required and/or an in-depth critique of one's own work.

If you are a graduate or a journalist or have some experience in writing beyond that of a hobby, then a Masters in Creative Writing might be more appropriate. We asked novelist and creative writing lecturer, Dr Paul Vlitos, about the degree course at the University of Surrey.

What does studying for a degree in creative writing entail?

At Surrey (and elsewhere) this usually involves producing a substantial portfolio of original creative writing over the course. Students are also required to 'reflect critically' on the writing process – to write an essay or essays about the work they've produced – what they were trying to achieve, putting their writing in generic/literary/historical/personal context, and reflecting on how the piece changed and developed during the writing process. Most creative writing courses at university are based on a workshop model, in which students first read and discuss a few key critical or creative texts related to a different theme each week – then have the chance to experiment in relation to the week's theme creatively in class by doing some writing of their own. Over the course people gain greatly in confidence through sharing and discussing their work with others in a supportive atmosphere, overseen by a published professional writer.

Does studying creative writing at university give students a realistic understanding of commercial publishing in the UK today, and are publishers themselves more favourably disposed to writers with creative writing degrees?

It is certainly important for all creative writing courses to emphasise that they cannot offer a 'magic ticket' to publication, fame and fortune. What courses can provide is a supportive and dedicated workshop setting to help people develop their writing. I'm not aware of any evidence of publishers favouring writers

*who have formal qualifications in creative writing –
although a qualification from a well-regarded
institution certainly might help a young writer stand
out from the crowd. One would also hope that with a
decent course the evidence would show in the writing.*

**How would you define literary fiction and how
does it differ from commercial or genre fiction?
These distinctions seem to matter to the
publishing industry, but should they matter?**

*I think you'd have to define them in terms of the type
of expectations that readers bring to a book – and the
rewards they expect from it. In that sense I think it
does make sense to think about writing (and how to
publish it) in terms of 'literary' vs
'commercial'/'genre' fiction.*

**Does the University of Surrey offer careers
advice to graduates of its creative writing
courses?**

*Yes, our BA course has an optional placement year,
which offers students the chance to experience the
world of work for themselves – and many of our
students use that to explore publishing and other
writing-related industries.*

**Does the university invite industry
professionals such as authors, agents and
publishers to come and talk to students?**

A solid creative writing course should also arrange visits from published writers and publishers to talk to their students. I'm very keen at the moment to get in an editor and have her talk through the editing process on a recent book with one of her authors – I think students and readers in general often have a hard time understanding quite how that relationship works.

If you examine your own circumstances, this will narrow the field when it comes to choosing the right course for you. If you have a full time job and/or family, a full time course is probably not going to be appropriate. Similarly, after you've found out what the fees for a degree will be, you might think twice about applying (although don't despair because depending on your circumstances help might be forthcoming).

If attending a face-to-face course is difficult, a correspondence course might prove to be more suitable. The Open College of Arts offers modules which can lead to a degree. The London School of Journalism offers a wide variety of well-established courses, including novel writing, writing romantic fiction and writing short stories.

More recently, the publishing industry itself has begun to offer courses in creative writing. The Faber Academy has the illustrious publishing house of the same name behind it. Legend Press is a smaller independent publisher which offers various services to authors, including workshops in creative writing.

Following your own path

Everyone's writing journey is unique, but each one is likely to be a long and winding road, rather than a quick nip down to the local shops. It will almost certainly be interesting and fun, but it's also likely to be arduous or even painful at times. You'll need to take with you the ability to learn and the energy and passion to keep going.

Your own writing vehicle can come in any shape or size. The world needs every sort, from delivery van to racing car. So now, imagine your body of work as a specific vehicle. What kind is it? Do you have a rusty old jalopy behind the house, rusty because you've invested a little here and a little there when you've had time, but mostly you've neglected it? Or are you constantly polishing your Bentley? Perhaps you have joined the Bentley owners' club, subscribe to *My Bentley* weekly and have taken the engine apart several times, re-sprayed the bodywork…in short, you are obsessed, and have brought all your talent and ingenuity together to make yours the best Bentley there could be.

But, even if this is the case, at some point you'll need fuel to take your Bentley on the road because you'll want to show it off to the public at a rally. This is when you'll need considerable energy of your own. You may have to push your Bentley to the petrol station. Then, having made it to the rally, you might find the main interest among the punters this year is E-type Jags. You had been hoping to sell your Bentley for shed-loads, but you were offered only a tiny sum. Do you consider modifying it into an amphibious Bentley and hope it will catch the imagination of a wealthy collector, or do you think of selling it on the Internet?

If you are writing for the edification and enjoyment of the next generation of your family, you may think you don't need to go on a creative writing course. You have access to all the research you need. But while there is a ready-made chronological structure to your work, it could still be worth learning the skills of characterisation and how to employ intrigue and jeopardy to encourage your reader to read on. A list of events doesn't usually make for a compelling story.

Do you want to win the Man Booker and/or sell a million? Whatever your goals, be decisive and keep them firmly in sight. Of course, however brilliant you are, you will need a considerable amount of luck. But imagine how annoyed you would be if luck came along and you weren't ready, or you were at home on your own when luck signed in at your local writing group.

You might be writing for your own personal pleasure, in which case you probably don't need to go on a course at all. Why give yourself potential grief? There are, no doubt, many secret diarists whose writing will never be made public. The simple act of putting pen to paper for their own entertainment is enough. But, for the majority of writers whose sentences wriggle so urgently into life, the need is to send their stories out into the wild and have them read.

Exercise

If you're not sure if a face-to-face course or distance learning course or no course is going to be right for you, think about how you learn best –

when you're working alone or when you're interacting with others?

Once you have decided, try doing the opposite and see how you feel about it. If you're a loner, pluck up the courage to talk to someone about your writing. If you lack confidence and don't tend to trust your own judgement, enter a writing competition *without* first getting feedback.

A professional writer has to be able to work alone *and* in a team situation.

CONCLUSION

Teaching And Learning

Perhaps you're now wondering about taking some one-to-one or class lessons in creative writing? You have lots of choices. You could take a course of lessons by distance learning, you could sign up for a face-to-face class, or you could arrange some private tutorials.

Distance learning is the most flexible option because you'll be able to work at your own speed and when your writing fits in with the rest of your life. As we've seen, the London School of Journalism offers several courses and has an impressive record of success, with many of its graduates becoming well-published short story writers, novelists and journalists. All the LSJ's tutors are professionals in their tutorial fields.

A face-to-face class run by a local authority, an independent organisation or an individual teacher will appeal to people who like to interact with others, see their reactions and hear what they have to say.

Many writers, especially novelists, find they end up leading fairly isolated lives, and some of them feel it can be good to see other people from time to time.

But some writers actually love being by themselves, alone at their desks, talking to their characters and writing their stories. These writers find the real world an irritating distraction, and they can happily spend weeks alone, never seeing or indeed wanting to see anyone else.

Writers' retreats are tailor-made for these modern day anchorites!

Private one-to-one tutorials are the most intense and also the most expensive learning option. But, if you get on well with your tutor, these might prove to be your fastest track to learning success. Your tutor will be able to concentrate on you, and you won't be held up while other students talk about work in which you might have no interest.

What should you look for in a teacher and how can you find one?

As with almost anything in life, it pays to ask around. If you join a writing group, face-to-face or online, you'll be able to get some feedback on the courses or classes other people have taken.

You'll find plenty of advertisements for classes and courses in magazines for writers such as *Mslexia, Writing Magazine* and *Writers' Forum*. Any reputable organisation or individual will explain what is involved and answer any questions you might have before you're asked to part with any money.

You should be suspicious of anyone who doesn't have an email address, website or other Internet presence, because these days writers – and certainly all teachers of creative writing – need to be able to use social networks. A retired English teacher who has no record of publication and no contacts in the publishing trade might be able to teach you the difference between *it's* and *its*, but he or she won't know what's going on in the real world of commercial publishing.

A good creative writing teacher will:

Listen to you
Motivate you

Inspire you

Identify your strengths and help you to build on them

Identify your weaknesses and help you to overcome them

Praise you when you succeed

Console you when you fail

Realise you don't need to hear about the teacher's own political or religious views, prejudices, assumptions, belief systems or neuroses. But the teacher should be willing to hear about any of your own which you wish to share, especially if these views and so on inform your work and help to explain you as an individual

Know how commercial publishing works – what a literary agent, publisher, commissioning editor, copy-editor, publicist and so on do – and be able to give you relevant guidance and information when you're sending work of your own to these parties

Get on with people and be interested in them

Be a writer too

What qualities do most teachers of creative

writing hope to find in their students?

A willingness to consider new concepts, suggestions, ideas and approaches to creative writing

A love of both reading and writing, especially in the genres for which the student is hoping to write successfully

A desire to learn from other writers as well as from the teacher

A curiosity about all kinds of creative writing and a desire to understand what makes or breaks any piece of work

A willingness to learn and understand the technical stuff – the bricklaying and wiring and plumbing aspects of writing

A willingness to experiment

An acceptance that some experiments will fail and a willingness to try to work out why they failed

An unquenchable optimism and determination to see a piece of work through to completion

What do they hope they *won't* find?

A habitual defensiveness which results in every or almost every suggestion the teacher makes being turned down
A refusal to listen to advice, even when paying for it
A determination to know best all the time
An inability to learn from example
A negative attitude to some commercially published work which is outside the student's own field of enjoyment and/or interest, and a failure to appreciate the fact that these authors must have got some things right. If they hadn't, no publisher would have been willing to spend considerable sums of money on them
A refusal to experiment
A pessimistic or paranoid outlook
A determination to believe there is a conspiracy to prevent the student being successful
A firm belief that there is some kind of magic key

Some yet-to-be-published writers often wonder if they need to know someone important in the world of writing, that's if they're to get anywhere

in their chosen profession. The answer is yes –
and no. It does help to know people who are
already published, so you could certainly try to
make friends with published authors by joining
organisations such as the Romantic Novelists'
Association or your own local writing group, and
by signing up to Facebook and Twitter.

You could also go to writing festivals and
conferences, where you will meet plenty of
writers, publishers, literary agents and people
interested in writing, all at different stages of
their careers.

All industry professionals are always on the
lookout for new writing talent. But talent is the
operative word. Beauty, contacts, money and
success in other fields won't help much unless
you also have writing talent.

As a student of creative writing, what do you need?

Time

A computer or word-processor or typewriter or notebook and pen (although if you want to submit anything to a commercial publisher, magazine editor or enter most competitions, it will need to be printed out on a computer)
A subject (or subjects) about which you wish to write, even if these are somewhat nebulous at the beginning of your creative writing life
Persistence
To believe that the only people who fail are those who give up

We're sure that if you can bring optimism, a willingness to learn and an open mind to your creative writing studies, you will have a good chance of succeeding in this hugely challenging, competitive but satisfying field.

Believe in yourself

Now you have read this book, we hope you will be more confident about your fiction writing skills. You will know what you should bear in mind when you are writing your own stories.

You will know how to be a good writer
You will also know how to be a good learner

You will also know how to be a good reader

We all learn by experimenting and by imitating –
by absorbing good habits by a kind of osmosis
and by putting what we've learned into practice.

So, whenever you read a story which really
impresses you, try to take a bit of time to work
out *why* you were so impressed.

Asking yourself the following questions should
help to get you started:

**Did you like or even love the central character
or characters?**
**Did you care what happened to them and were
you sad when it was time to say goodbye?**
**What about narrative viewpoint – did the author
choose the right viewpoint(s) and, as you read
the story, were you inside the heads of the
character(s) you liked best?**
**Did the story have a beginning which engaged
your attention?**
**Did the middle part develop the central conflict
situation and pull you even deeper into the
story?**
**Did the ending satisfy you and did you feel it
was the right one?**
Did you like listening to the characters?
**Did the dialogue sound natural, did it reveal
character to you, and did it move the story on?**

You'll probably find a story which you have enjoyed will tick most of these boxes.

Your challenge now is to get your reader to tick these boxes as he or she reads your own work.

We're confident you can do it!

Exercise

Make a list of your writing goals. Be realistic but also optimistic. What do you want to have achieved by this time next year? Maybe to have written half a dozen short stories? Or half the first draft of a novel?

Try to write every day, even if you manage only a hundred or so words. Why not get started by writing those first hundred words right now?

About the Authors

Cathie Hartigan grew up in London, but after studying at Dartington College of Arts, made Devon her home. An award-winning short story writer, she lectured in creative writing at Exeter College for nine years and is the current chair of Exeter Writers - http://www.exeterwriters.org.uk She is the founder and director of *CreativeWritingMatters*. http://www.creativewritingmatters.co.uk/ You can follow Cathie on Twitter at https://twitter.com/cathiehartigan or on Facebook at https://www.facebook.com/cathie.hartigan?ref=ts&fref=ts.

Margaret James grew up in Hereford and has lived in London, Oxford and Berkshire. She moved to Devon in 2002. She is the author of several contemporary and historical novels, a journalist working for the UK's *Writing Magazine*, and she teaches creative writing for the London School of Journalism.

She has a blog at
www.margaretjamesblog.blogspot.com and you
can follow Margaret on Twitter at
https://twitter.com/majanovelist or on Facebook
at
https://www.facebook.com/margaret.james.526
8?fref=ts
Find out more about her published fiction by
accessing her Author Central page at
www.amazon.co.uk.

.

Printed in Great Britain
by Amazon